## Mel Bay Presents

# AARON SHEARER

## Learning the Classic Guitar

# Part 1: Technique

edited by Tom Poore

To my many students with whom I
have shared the joy of learning —
whose enthusiasm and trust have provided
steadfast inspiration over the years.

# Acknowledgments

Writing the three books which constitute *Learning the Classic Guitar* has occupied the past two decades. During this time, so many people have offered encouragement that it would be impossible for me to list them all. A few people, however, have been especially supportive, and I'd like to express my gratitude to each of them by name:

To Ray Chester — former pupil, former colleague at Peabody Conservatory of Music, and steadfast friend. Throughout the many years of our association, he's always believed that guitar instruction needed to improve, and that these books needed to be written.

To Larry Alan Smith, Dean of Music at The North Carolina School of the Arts. Through his kind consideration, I've been spared the pressure of administrative duties which would have taken time from my research and writing. He's also been a source of gracious and unfailing support.

To Paul Grove, Leigh Mamlin, Sally Hirsh, and Richard Matteson for reading the manuscript, and for their suggestions and encouragement.

To the Semans Art Fund for its timely grant, which has eased the financial sting of completing the illustrations.

To Kathleen O'Brien, for her expertise and kind cooperation as illustrator.

To Alan Hirsh, who composed most of the music for *Part Two*. His contributions extend far past that of composer. Alan's suggestions, enthusiasm, and encouragement have been invaluable.

To Tom Poore, whose contribution has been more than that of editor. Our many hours of discussion helped to clarify my concepts, and occasionally uncovered a new idea which might have otherwise lain fallow.

And, finally, my heartfelt gratitude goes to my beloved wife, Lorraine, for reading and correcting the manuscript at its various stages, but most of all for her steadfast and loving support.

# Contents

∾    ∾    ∾    ∾    ∾    ∾    ∾

# Preface

Playing a musical instrument such as the classic guitar is one of the most remarkable of human achievements. The sustained concentration and skillful movements required to play proficiently are probably unsurpassed by any other human endeavor. My own *Classic Guitar Technique* series, written many years ago, was intended to aid in the development of these intellectual and physical skills.

In 1959, when the first of these books appeared, I was making a modest living as a guitar teacher in Washington, D.C. Ten years earlier I had experienced a devastating attack of tendonitis in my right hand, leaving me with only limited playing ability and no hope of ever earning a living as a performer. I little realized then that this crippling handicap would become a positive force in my life. It eventually prompted me to rethink the usual approach to learning the guitar. Could students learn the guitar more securely and efficiently? Could they avoid injuring the muscles and nerves of their hands as I had done? *Classic Guitar Technique, Volume I,* was the early result of my thinking, and I wrote it mainly to fill my own needs as a teacher.

Getting the book published was a formidable task. Andres Segovia was gracious enough to evaluate my manuscript but regretfully informed me that it was "totally worthless." Through the kind recommendation of Vladimir Bobri, however, the Ricordi Firm in New York consented to read my manuscript and eventually accepted it for publication.

The guitar community's interest in the book and its related volumes came slowly at first, and never in my most optimistic moments did I dream that the books would someday be used so extensively. Through their success, I was invited along with Sophocles Papas to join the faculty at American University in Washington, D.C. Together we inaugurated what I believe was the first major university degree program for guitar in the United States. A few years later I began a similar program at Catholic University of America, also in Washington, D.C. This was followed by the first degree program at a major conservatory, Peabody Conservatory of Music in Baltimore, Maryland, where I taught for 16 years. Since 1981 I've directed the guitar program at the North Carolina School of the Arts in Winston-Salem.

Over the years I have met a wide variety of talented people, many of whom have inspired me to seek a more effective approach to teaching the guitar. While my earlier books have proven beneficial, and some will continue to be useful, my approach to guitar study has advanced significantly. Through *Learning the Classic Guitar*, I hope to share these advances with anyone possessing a sincere interest in the guitar.

Students attempting to master the guitar face a challenging task. If they are to realize their goals, they should not waste time in unrewarding and potentially harmful study. Thus, I have sought concepts and procedures which, if carefully applied, will enable students to work more efficiently — resulting in the most secure and rewarding progress for the time they devote to study and practice.

In retrospect, it seems to have taken me far too long to arrive at these concepts and procedures. But after more than fifty years of teaching, I am gratified to see my students progressing more directly toward their goals. Further, many of these concepts are applicable not only to learning the guitar, but to the learning of other instruments as well, and I hope that someday all musicians will fully understand their importance.

Aaron Shearer
Winston-Salem, N.C.

# Introduction

Although learning any musical instrument is not easy, the classic guitar seems to be especially challenging. Because it offers so many possibilities for mistaken approaches, the guitar often proves confusing to students. In both technique and musical development, what initially appears easiest and most natural often turns out to be incorrect. Thus, to ensure that students avoid confusion, frustration, and wasted time, a *detailed* and *gradual* approach is essential. The better organized a challenging subject is, the more accessible it becomes.

Many ideas in my approach challenge traditional methods and assumptions. Although I have occasionally explained why I do things differently, I have not tried to give a point-by-point refutation of traditional guitar instruction. If my approach has value, it will stand on its own merits. The ultimate verdict will rest with the students and teachers who use these books.

There are five major areas in classic guitar study: technique, reading music, memorizing music, interpretation, and performance. Thus, the three parts of *Learning the Classic Guitar* are arranged as follows:

### Part One: Technique

This volume focuses on technical development, and it also provides crucial information about efficient study and practice. It will guide your development of the four essentials of technique: accuracy, strength, speed, and endurance.

### Part Two: Reading and Memorizing Music

This volume presents the elements of music, and procedures for developing your ability to sightread and memorize. It also introduces a systematic way to learn written notes rapidly and correlate them with their locations on the fingerboard.

### Part Three: Music Interpretation and Performance

This volume helps you form clear and accurate concepts of musical expression. It also provides information on learning how to perform for others with security and confidence.

# *Using These Books*

These books are designed to help you at whatever your level of accomplishment. If you're a beginner, of course, you'll start at the beginning and develop gradually. But even if you already play, you still should start at the beginning of this book, where you'll find important basic information. Proceed carefully, and you'll begin to discover and progressively solve the problems which have held you back — this is the most efficient way to fill the gaps in your training.

In developing these books, I've adhered to the following concepts:

> • *How and what students practice is as important as how much they practice.* Students should be aware that they are developing habits of thought and movement. These habits can be either harmful or beneficial. To develop beneficial habits, students must have clear goals and sufficient information about how to proceed.
>
> • *Give information only when it's immediately useful.* Students tend to forget information they can't soon apply.
>
> • *Start with the easiest skills.* Give students tasks which they can learn within a reasonable period of time. For example, most guitar books (including one of my own earlier books) start right-hand training with finger alternation. Alternation, however, is a very difficult movement for beginners, and should be introduced only after sufficient preparation. Further, it's much easier to begin right-hand training with the thumb rather than the fingers. Beginning with the thumb affords more secure access to the three open strings of the G-major triad (G, B, D). Thus, students can start playing music almost immediately — an important consideration for eager beginners who want to get a taste of playing the guitar.
>
> • *Approach challenging skills gradually.* Students who are given complex tasks without sufficient preparation often become frustrated and give up. Others persistently push through their confusion and acquire bad habits. When material is arranged in a gradual manner, both these possibilities are avoided.

You should use *Part One* and *Part Two* together. This allows you to simultaneously develop your technique and music reading. Begin *Part Three* as soon as you can confidently play short pieces.

Carefully observe the text. If it's italicized, capitalized, or otherwise highlighted, it's especially important. Also, observe any repeated information. It's repeated because I've found that certain things need to be emphasized to keep students on the right track.

These books are practical guides to learning the guitar. Thus, you can't expect simply to read through them and immediately understand every procedure. You need to work carefully with this information, discovering how it best fits your needs. Be assured, however, that the information in these books has been successfully used by many students. With patient study and practice, you too will find it rewarding.

A caution to teachers: Although understanding is the key to efficient progress, students vary in their ability to understand. Students of any age — especially children — should never be burdened with information they can't understand and quickly apply. The younger the student, the more "doing" should be stressed. Experienced students involved in remedial study, however, need the fullest possible understanding of "how" and "why" before beginning to practice.

# The Classic Guitar

The guitar family can be divided into two distinct groups: those strung with nylon strings and those strung with steel strings. Nylon strings are usually sounded with the right-hand fingers, while steel strings are usually sounded with a plectrum.

The nylon-string guitar produces sound acoustically through a resonating chamber. The steel-string guitar produces sound through either a resonating chamber or electronic amplification. The steel-string guitar is used mainly for popular, folk, and country music. Although the nylon-string guitar can be used for all kinds of music, it's most commonly used in playing classical music.

## "Classic" or "Classical" Guitar?

The nylon-string guitar is commonly known by two related names: the classic guitar and the classical guitar. Since both names adequately distinguish this guitar from its steel-string relative, I readily accept either. Thus, using one term or the other has never been a major issue with me. As many guitarists have done, however, I've chosen one term in preference to the other. The following are my reasons.

"Classical guitar" may have arisen because much of the guitar's early development and repertoire dates from the Classical period of music (1750-1830). Granted, the guitar does have important roots in the Classical period. The overall design and construction of the modern guitar, however, was developed by Antonio Torres (1817-1892). His remarkable innovations date from about 1850 — well after the Classical period ended. Further, "classical" can be misleading, suggesting that this type of guitar is suited only for classical music.

To me, "classic guitar" seems more appropriate. According to *Webster's Dictionary*, classic means "of recognized value: serving as a standard of excellence; traditional, enduring." Also, the term "classic" is somewhat more distinctive than "classical." There are many pieces of music that date from the Classical period which have never become classics. Something becomes classic through the test of time. Thus, it's accurate to say that, among the various types of guitar, ours is the "classic" guitar.

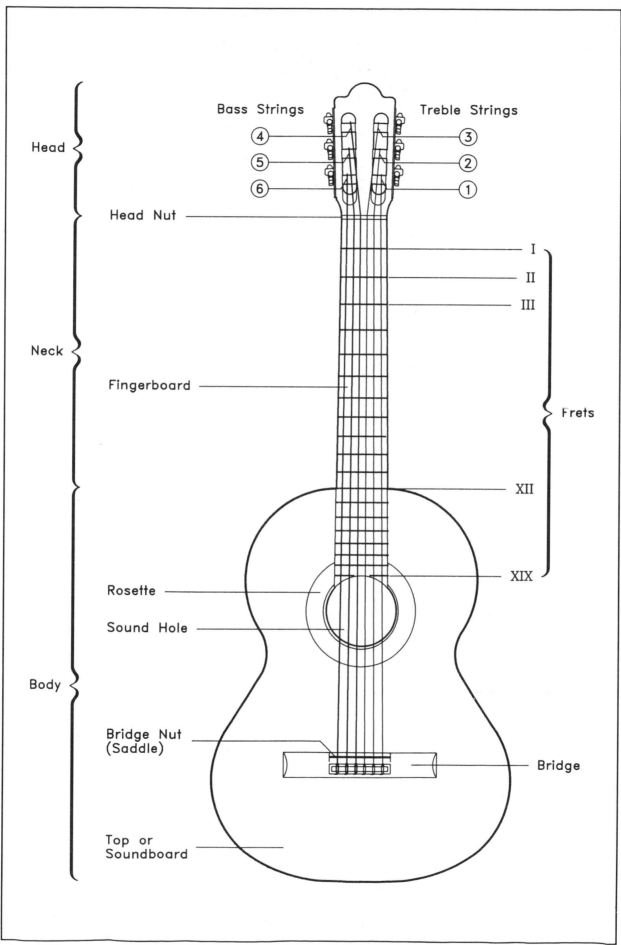

*Figure 1A: The classic guitar.*

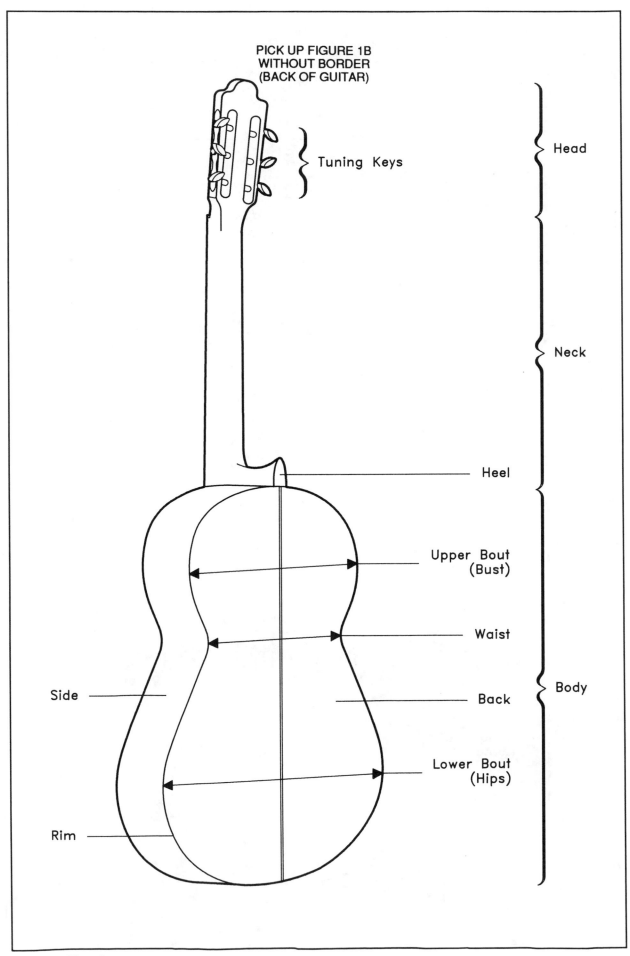

*Figure 1B: The guitar.*

## ATTACHING THE STRINGS

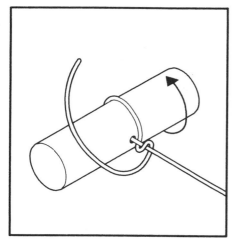 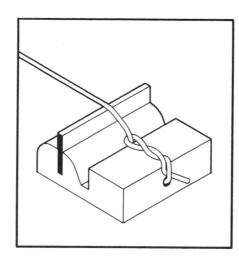 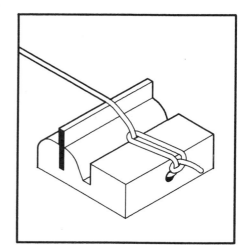

*Figures 2A, 2B, 2C*

Figure 2A shows how to attach a string to a roller pin. Figures 2B and 2C show two common ways of attaching a string to the bridge. **NOTE:** When attaching a string to the bridge, be sure that the last turn of the string end is secured behind the back edge of the bridge — this will prevent the string from slipping when it's brought up to pitch.

# Tuning the Guitar

It takes considerable practice to tune the guitar quickly and accurately. You must train your ear to detect the slightest differences in pitch. If you have no musical training, ask a qualified teacher or musician (not necessarily a guitarist) to help you tune your guitar.

The names of the six strings are E or first (the lightest gauge or smallest in diameter, and highest in pitch), B or second, G or third, D or fourth, A or fifth, and E or sixth (the heaviest gauge and lowest in pitch). The pitches of the six guitar strings are found on the piano as shown in Figure 3.

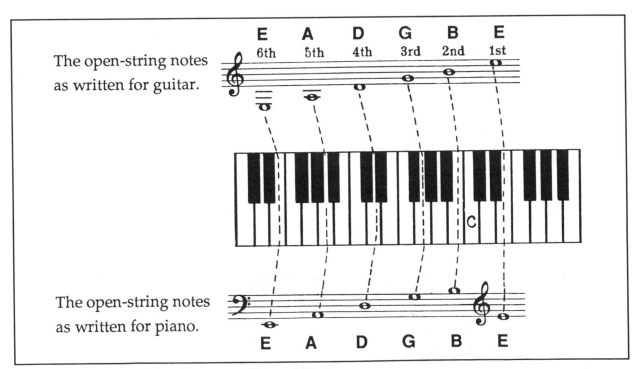

*Figure 3: Notice that five of the strings are tuned below middle C.*

You should keep the guitar tuned to standard pitch. The most common source for obtaining standard pitch is a tuning fork which produces 440 vibrations per second, sounding the tone "A." This A is obtained on the guitar by depressing the E or first string at the 5th fret.

Another method of tuning is with the aid of an electronic device designed for measuring the pitch of each guitar string. This enables you to tune visually — you simply adjust the string until the device indicates that the string is perfectly tuned.

When tuning, loosen the string to a point slightly below the desired pitch, then bring it up to pitch. This will take up any slack in the gear mechanism of the tuning keys.

Once you've tuned the guitar to standard pitch, you must ensure that the guitar is in tune with itself by checking each string against its adjacent string. The following diagram shows you how to do this:

1) To find the correct pitch of the fifth string, depress the sixth string at the 5th fret.
2) To find the correct pitch of the fourth string, depress the fifth string at the 5th fret.
3) To find the correct pitch of the third string, depress the fourth string at the 5th fret.
4) To find the correct pitch of the second string, depress the third string at the 4th fret.
5) To find the correct pitch of the first string, depress the second string at the 5th fret.

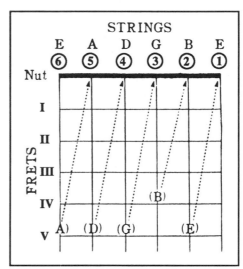

Figure 4

(If you use a tuning fork to establish the pitch of A at the 5th fret of the first string, you'll need to reverse this procedure — begin tuning with the first string and end with the sixth.)

After you've tuned your guitar, make a final test by playing the E major chord:

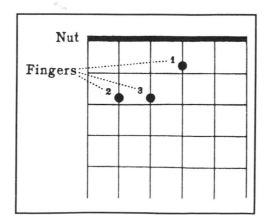

With your left-hand fingers in the positions indicated, hold the three strings firmly against the frets. Using your right-hand thumb, strum all six strings, beginning with the sixth. Keep your thumb quite relaxed, and allow it to glide slowly from one string to the other until all the strings are ringing clearly. If the strings are properly tuned, the E major chord is one of the most beautiful chords on the guitar. It should have a thoroughly pleasant sound, with no feeling of discord. With a little practice, you'll be able to tell if a particular string is out of tune merely by slowly strumming the E major chord and listening to each tone as it's sounded.

Be sure that your guitar is always properly tuned as you practice. By learning to tune your guitar precisely, you'll not only ensure a true pitch in performance, you'll also be making substantial progress toward becoming a musician.

# Playing Condition of the Guitar

It's important that you consider the playing condition of the guitar you intend to use. If the guitar has a warped neck or is inaccurately adjusted, it will be difficult or impossible to play. The few minutes you spend determining a guitar's playing condition may save you considerable expense and many hours of unrewarding study.

*Before you can accurately test the playing condition of any guitar, the instrument must first be tuned to standard pitch.*

Test a guitar for a warped or bent neck in the following manner:

❑ **Depress the E or first string at the 1st and 15th frets simultaneously. Held firmly in this manner, the string should appear to almost touch each intervening fret. Then follow the same procedure with the E or sixth string. If either string doesn't almost touch each intervening fret, the neck is warped. The guitar may need a new fingerboard, or the neck may need to be reset.**

## Determining the Action of a Guitar

*Action* is the distance of the strings above the frets. A guitar's action strongly affects its playability. If the strings are set too high, you'll find it difficult to press them firmly against the frets — this is referred to as a "high" or "hard" action. If the strings are set too low, they'll vibrate against the frets and produce harsh buzzing sounds — this is referred to as a "low" or "soft" action. A guitar with inaccurately adjusted action can be difficult or even impossible to play.

Your guitar should have an action that's neither too high nor too low — the strings shouldn't be too hard to press firmly against the frets, yet they must produce a clear tone with maximum volume. Excellent materials and craftsmanship don't necessarily indicate that a guitar is well adjusted. Many new guitars —even quite expensive ones — aren't in the best playing condition because they haven't been properly adjusted. But any well-constructed guitar which doesn't have a warped neck can usually be adjusted by raising or lowering its bridge saddle, its head nut, or both.

The following is an accurate method of determining whether the action is in reasonably good adjustment:

### STEP ONE: Checking the Bridge Saddle Height

❑ With the E or first string held firmly against the 1st fret, this string should be no less than 3/32" above the top of the 12th fret.

❑ Measuring in the same manner, the E or sixth string should be no less than 1/8" above the top of the 12th fret.

❑ The second, third, fourth, and fifth strings must be on a level plane between the first and sixth.

(Because of their wide vibrations, the heavier gauge strings should have a higher action.)

### STEP TWO: Checking the Head Nut Height

Use a standard automotive gap gauge to measure the distance between the strings and the 1st fret.

❑ In open position, the distance between the top of the first fret and the first two strings should be .025".

❑ The third, fourth, fifth, and sixth strings should be .030" above the 1st fret.

If the guitar requires an adjustment of its action, take it to a reputable stringed instrument repair shop for correction.

These specifications produce a medium-low action, suitable for the average student. As your playing ability and knowledge of the guitar develop, you may desire a slightly higher action:

- **First string: 1/8" (instead of 3/32")**

- **Sixth string: 5/32" (instead of 1/8")**

You should determine the fine points of action adjustment in accordance with your individual requirements and the characteristics of a particular instrument. You shouldn't, however, try an action *lower* than specified in the previous procedure —if set any lower, the strings will tend to vibrate against the frets.

# Choosing a Teacher

Like other major instruments, the classic guitar has advanced beyond the days when a self-taught player could become a concert artist. If you want to master the guitar, you need a competent teacher. Even if you have modest goals, you can reach them more quickly and easily with a teacher's guidance. The principles and ideas in these books are extremely important, but applying them most effectively can be done only with the aid of a teacher.

Good teachers help schedule the introduction of new material and explain its meaning. They encourage you when you're on the right track, and quickly correct you when you go wrong. They show you how to study efficiently and effectively. They build your confidence. In short, a competent teacher will take you far beyond what you could accomplish on your own.

But how do you find a competent teacher? Guitar teachers aren't licensed or regulated. Anyone who wants to teach the guitar can do so, and the number of competent teachers is limited. So how can a student — particularly a beginner — accurately evaluate a teacher?

Fortunately there are guidelines you'll find helpful. Before you begin looking for a teacher, read "Approaching Guitar Study," (pp. 1–8). Become thoroughly familiar with the concepts in this section. Then talk with your prospective teacher. Ask the teacher about his or her approach to teaching the guitar, and listen for the following:

- **Does the teacher emphasize performance -the act of sharing music with others- as the goal of guitar study?**

- **Does the teacher discuss the extreme importance of habits in guitar playing?**

- **Does the teacher emphasize avoiding confusion and error?**

- **Does the teacher talk about developing security and confidence?**

Bear in mind, these concepts aren't simply my opinions of how the guitar should be taught. They're basic concepts of how everyone can learn and develop as rapidly and securely as possible. Your teacher had better know and emphasize them.

When choosing a teacher, remember the following:

• *Be wary of teachers who recommend the "natural" approach to learning the guitar.* There is a natural approach to learning the guitar, but it isn't what many teachers think it is. (See "The Natural Approach," p. 117.)

• *Beware of teachers who say "Get all the information you can from all the sources you can, then decide for yourself what's right."* You have no basis for evaluating information. That's the teacher's job.

• *Don't judge a teacher only by his or her students.* Many teachers are better at attracting talented students than teaching them, and some talented students learn to play quite well despite having an incompetent teacher. Also, a young competent teacher may not yet have built a reputation which attracts the best students.

• *Don't judge a teacher only by his or her playing.* Many people assume that an excellent player is also an excellent teacher. In reality, however, performing artists are often poor teachers. Teaching and playing are two entirely different skills, and an excellent teacher may have only modest ability as a player.

• *Don't assume that a teacher is competent simply because he or she has a degree from a prestigious university or conservatory.* Nor should you assume that a teacher is competent simply because he or she is teaching at a prestigious university or conservatory.

Don't stop evaluating your teacher after you've begun taking lessons, particularly if you're not making progress within reasonable time. Beware of teachers who rely almost entirely on demonstration, expecting you to learn mainly through imitation. Also beware of teachers who, instead of showing you how to work more effectively, insist that you're not working hard enough, even though you're practicing several hours a day. Trust your instincts — too many students ignore their better judgment and stay with an unsatisfactory teacher.

Bear in mind, an incompetent teacher can hinder your development and ultimately cripple your ability to play the guitar. If you're not progressing in spite of your best efforts, find another teacher.

# Approaching Guitar Study

Perhaps you're just beginning the guitar — you're attracted to its sound, and it appears relatively easy to learn. But you've tried to play a few chords or a simple melody, and you've found the guitar isn't as easy as it appears. So you realize that you need information, and you're ready to begin learning.

Or perhaps you already play the guitar. You've studied on your own or with a teacher for some time, and you've even built a modest repertoire. But you're dissatisfied with your playing. Your performances are disturbingly erratic, and they don't seem to improve regardless of how much you practice. You need a better approach, and you're eager to find it.[†]

But whatever your level of accomplishment, there are basic concepts of learning which you need to know. Certain things you can think about are beneficial to your playing. Other things are so harmful that the more you practice, the further you'll get from ever playing well. Thus, to learn the guitar as efficiently as possible, you need to know what to emphasize and what to avoid.

## Your Goal: Sharing Music

There may be as many reasons for learning the classic guitar as there are guitarists. Perhaps you're attracted to its music, or maybe you're lured by the challenge of playing this beautiful instrument. Perhaps the refinement of the classic guitar appeals to you. But whatever your initial reasons for learning to play, there's a single goal which encompasses all areas of guitar study. This goal is eloquently stated in the following quotation which I came across many years ago:

---

[†]If you're an experienced player, see "The Remedial Student," p. 113.

*"Strange is our situation here upon earth. Each of us comes for a short visit, not knowing why, but sometimes seeming to divine a purpose. From the standpoint of daily life, however, there is one thing we do know, that we are here for the sake of others — above all for those upon whose smile and well-being our own happiness depends, but also for the countless unknown souls with whose fate we are attached by a bond of sympathy. Many times a day I realize how much my own outer and inner life is built upon the efforts of my fellow men, both living and dead, and how earnestly I must exert myself in order to give in return as much as I have received."*

*Albert Einstein*

"For the sake of others." These words sparked a flame in my imagination which has endured to this day. They've been a stabilizing force for me during difficult times, and have strongly contributed to my generally rewarding life. But they also suggest something more: They give each of us a purpose and motivation for playing the guitar.

Music is for sharing. This is why you're learning the guitar. Playing music is an especially rewarding way to satisfy your deep natural drive to share with others.

Of course, you also want to play for personal enjoyment. But consider the following: Imagine that you're given the finest guitar, a complete music library, and all the time you wish for practice. However, there's one stipulation: you must always play alone in a soundproof room. If no one would ever hear you, how long would you continue to play the guitar?

We simply don't play only for ourselves. There's always an imaginary audience at least dimly present as we practice and play. *Thus, by recognizing that performance is your goal, you'll carefully avoid forming any habit of thought or movement which you don't want to occur during a performance.*

# Essentials for Performance

> •*Security:* This encompasses the two basic aims of technical and musical study:
>
> 1. *Accuracy:* playing without missed or flubbed notes; it also includes intended fingerings, tone, and interpretation.
>
> 2. *Continuity:* playing the piece from start to finish without hesitations.
>
> •*Confidence:* This encompasses your emotional and intellectual outlook. Based on experience, you believe that you can securely perform for others.

*Any lack of security and confidence will hinder or even nullify your technique and musicianship.*

# Avoiding Habits of Confusion and Error

You'll play the guitar through the habits of thought and movement acquired in your daily study and practice. Your ability to perform with security and confidence will be powerfully influenced by these habits. Inevitably, you'll acquire either habits of confusion and error or habits of understanding, concentration, and accuracy.

Although we have a natural ability to learn basic activities such as walking or throwing, we have no such aptitude for playing the guitar — the coordination required is far beyond our normal experience. Thus, some confusion and error will occur in the early stages of your training. But from the beginning, you must learn to minimize confusion and error — never allow them to persist beyond the early stages of your training.

*Always remember, during every minute of practice you're acquiring habits that will determine how well you'll eventually play. If you're confused and making errors as you practice, confusion and error will unavoidably become part of your playing.*

To understand how confusion and error can influence your playing, consider what happens when you begin learning a new finger movement. First, you tend to become confused. This is inevitable and, by itself, not immediately harmful. But if you allow confusion to persist, consider what happens next: You make errors, and you try to overcome them by repeating the movement again and again.

Meanwhile, what's happening to your muscles? Muscles don't make value judgments — they don't reject inaccurate repetitions and concentrate only on accurate ones. If you make insecure and error-filled repetitions, your muscles will acquire insecure and error-filled habits of movement. If you make secure and error-free repetitions, your muscles will acquire secure and error-free habits of movement.

*In acquiring habits of movement, muscles respond to repetition — that's all they can do. Thus, you must practice in a way which minimizes error-filled repetitions and maximizes accurate repetitions.*

# Aim-Directed Movement

Clearly, confusion and error are devastating to your development as a guitarist. They're also the prime cause of performance anxiety. Through misguided training, many gifted guitarists have ingrained confusion and error into their playing. Consequently, they never know what it's like to perform with security and confidence.

*Aim-Directed Movement (ADM)* is a positive way to avoid confusion and error. The essence of ADM is this: *knowing where and how to move before moving — seeing in your mind's eye the movements you'll make on the guitar before you actually make them.*

You'll apply ADM when learning new *movement forms.* A movement form is the shape or pattern of one complete movement. In sounding a string with a right-hand finger, for example, approaching the string, sounding the string, and following through constitute one complete movement form. Further, a rapid and unified succession of notes played with either hand will be felt as a single movement form. When guitarists play music, they're actually executing a series of individual movement forms. Thus, the more movement forms you can accurately play by habit, the more accessible all music becomes.

In learning a new movement form, be aware that ADM has two phases:

> • **Preparation:** You clarify and understand a movement form as fully as possible <u>before</u> playing it on the guitar. Thorough preparation gives you clear aims for carrying out the movement.
>
> • **Application:** You play the movement form on the guitar as accurately as possible, seeing your finger movements in your mind's eye an instant before you actually execute them. Your goal is to accurately repeat the movement form until it becomes a secure habit.

By applying ADM, you avoid the faulty habits acquired through rote repetition. In rote repetition, students begin with inaccuracy and try to work their way to accuracy. Since their muscles make no distinction between accurate and inaccurate repetitions, these students must constantly try to replace the faulty habits ingrained by their early inaccurate repetitions. With ADM, you begin with accurate repetitions, so you don't waste time trying to replace faulty habits. Thus, <u>ADM is a method of building secure habits quickly and efficiently.</u>

# Developing Sustained Concentration

In all areas of guitar study, the practical and effective application of information depends on your ability to concentrate. Your hands can only respond to your mind — what you think, they do. *Thus, you need to maintain the sharpest possible concentration as you practice.*

Learn to recognize the enemies of concentration:

- **Confusion**
- **Anxiety**
- **Boredom**
- **Fatigue**

You should work gradually enough so that you can master a given procedure within a reasonable period of time. If the material is too difficult, you'll have to repeat it for so long that you'll become bored and fatigued. Also, <u>if you don't have a clear aim, your concentration will suffer.</u> Don't begin practicing until you clearly understand what you're trying to achieve.

6

*Beware of the wandering mind!* Be sensitive to when your attention begins to wane, and take a short break when necessary. If you find that you still can't concentrate, set the guitar aside. Do something different to clear your mind —perform some vigorous exercise or take a short walk.

## Guidelines for Study and Practice

• *Always practice with a definite aim:* Your muscles require clear direction. If you try to play without clear aims, you'll acquire stubborn habits of confusion and error that are difficult to replace. Practicing with an aim helps to avoid confusion and error at all levels of guitar study, including interpretation and performance.

• *Carefully study each directive until you clearly understand it:* Don't attempt something on the guitar until you clearly understand your aim. Then, with the guitar, experiment to discover how the aim can be effectively carried out.

• *Acquire the habit of sustained concentration:* Your security in all aspects of guitar study depends on how well you concentrate during your practice sessions. Practicing when you're not concentrating sufficiently is worse than no practice at all — it's better to set aside the guitar until you can concentrate clearly.

• *Proceed one step at a time:* Avoid rushing ahead. Carefully clarify and practice each aim before approaching the next. Isolate any movement form or position which needs improvement. Practice each movement form until it becomes a secure habit.

• *Don't expect to feel comfortable with the guitar at first:* Remember, the guitar presents unfamiliar problems of coordination. You'll need time to train your muscles. Control, accuracy, and increased confidence will tell you that you're developing secure coordination.

> **• Don't expect to immediately retain all that you achieved during your last practice session:** You're developing habits of correct movement and positioning, and it may take several sessions before a movement form or position becomes habitual. Review what you previously learned before beginning new material.
>
> **• Challenge yourself:** For the quickest progress, be constantly aware of your limitations and work to correct them. Don't simply repeat what's easy — push yourself to the limits of what you can do without confusion and error.
>
> **• Maintain a balanced approach:** Be thorough. Don't let some areas of your development lag behind others.
>
> **• Remember that sufficient preparation and training are all that stand between you and the ability to play the guitar:** Set high goals, and be persistent. Until you try, you'll never know your potential for sharing music with others.

## Summary

You may have doubts as you begin learning the guitar. Everyone's musical talent varies, so naturally you wonder about your own. Can you really learn to play the guitar? Do you have the talent to play well?

Be assured. While the extent of your musical talent may still be a mystery, there's nothing mysterious about learning to play the guitar. Anyone who has the desire can learn. In fact, people with lesser talent who pursue well-directed study often surpass talented people who study badly. Your attitude and approach are more important than your musical talent.

Be positive. You'll encounter many new ideas in this book. Anytime you offhandedly reject ideas before giving them a chance to work, you also reject the benefits of those ideas. Frustration, impatience, and a closed mind will only impede your progress. A positive attitude saves time — it promotes objectivity, allowing you to tentatively accept and apply new information.

You'll learn the guitar through personal experimentation and discovery. But your experimentation must never be random. To experiment most effectively, always remember the following as you study and practice:

> • *Keep performance as your goal:* Do not form any habit during practice which you don't want to occur in performance.
>
> • *Build habits of security and confidence:* These are essential for performing. You must build secure habits of thought and movement.
>
> • *Precede each movement you make on the guitar with a clear aim:* This is the most efficient way to develop correct habits of thought and movement.
>
> • *Develop the habit of sustained concentration:* The sharper and clearer your concentration, the more secure and efficient your progress will be. If you're not concentrating well, don't practice!
>
> • *Avoid confusion and error:* Confusion and error are fatal to your concentration, and thus will hinder all areas of your study.

# The Four Principles of Efficient Muscle Function

Muscular exertion is essential for all body positioning and movement. You normally feel and identify this exertion as tension. In guitar playing, tension can be either productive or counterproductive. *Productive tension* is the minimum muscular exertion needed to play the guitar. It signals that your muscles are coordinating efficiently and harmoniously. *Counterproductive tension* is excessive muscular exertion which impedes guitar playing. It signals that your muscles are not properly coordinating.

But how do you recognize counterproductive tension? If you're a beginner, every new position and movement will feel tense — if you're an experienced player, you may be so accustomed to counterproductive tension that you don't recognize it. Thus, until you've gained experience in recognizing counterproductive tension, you'll need to rely on objective standards for determining muscular efficiency.

The Principles of Efficient Muscle Function provide you with these objective standards. Simply stated, these principles describe how muscles function with the least exertion — accomplishing the most work with the least tension.

Before introducing the principles, we need to define two terms:

*Flexion:* At any finger joint, flexion is movement toward the palm. At any thumb joint, flexion is movement toward the opposite side of the palm. Flexion is controlled by the flexor muscles.

*Extension:* At any finger or thumb joint, extension is movement away from the palm. Extension is controlled by the extensor muscles.[†]

---

[†]In scientific terms, the thumb movements are called "adduction" and "abduction." To avoid complication, however, the terms "extension" and "flexion" will suffice for our purposes.

The Four Principles of Efficient Muscle Function are as follows — each functions interdependently with the others:

> ***Muscular Alignment:*** **Muscles function most efficiently only when naturally aligned with their base and joint attachments. Natural alignment provides the most direct pull of the muscles which control your back, wrist, and finger joints.**
>
> ***Midrange Function of Joints:*** **Muscles function most efficiently only when the joints they control are operated within their midrange of movement. Midrange positioning and movement provides optimum leverage to the muscles involved.[†]**
>
> ***Uniform Direction of Joint Movement:*** **Muscles function most efficiently only when all three joints of a finger or the thumb are either flexed or extended together. In contrast to flexing one joint while extending another, simultaneous extension or flexion simplifies coordination of the muscles.**
>
> ***Follow-Through:*** **Muscles function most efficiently only when there is sufficient follow-through to avoid a build-up of counterproductive tension. Sufficient follow-through means that, once a movement has been initiated, no *intentional* restraint is applied to the movement.[††]**

Another important consideration, though not involving the mechanics of movement, strongly influences muscle function:

***Muscles function most efficiently only when the mind is free of anxiety.*** In practice or performance, anxiety causes counterproductive tension which inhibits the ability of the muscles to function efficiently.

---

[†]For an explanation of midrange, see p. 31.

[††]For a practical demonstration of this principle, see p. 122.

# *Summary*

In playing the guitar, you can't always fully conform to these principles. You can, however, establish a basic technique which takes advantage of the movements and positions that cause the least counterproductive tension. Thus, the Principles of Efficient Muscle Function give you objective standards for recognizing these positions and movements.

Always observe the following as you learn a new position or movement form:

---

- **Have a definite aim of positioning or movement.**

- **Use the Principles of Efficient Muscle Function to provide maximum advantage for the involved muscles.**

- **Maintain the position or repeat the movement accurately and without confusion or anxiety.**

---

Under these ideal conditions, the number of repetitions you'll need to develop sufficient coordination depends on your physical aptitude, your ability to concentrate, the complexity of the movement, and the level of skill you wish to achieve.

# Positioning the Guitar

Positioning the guitar is the foundation of your technical development. You need to establish a position which is effective and enables you to avoid counterproductive tension. Excess tension in your back and shoulders automatically spreads to your arms and hands, reducing your sensitivity to movement and hindering your development of coordination.

> • **Your general aim is to hold the guitar in the most effective, comfortable, and secure playing position, providing free access to the strings and to the full range of the fingerboard.**

For your position to be comfortable, your back muscles must be aligned and your shoulders level. Thus, positioning the guitar involves the Muscular Alignment Principle.

## *General Positioning*

Figure 6 illustrates the general seating position. Carefully study this illustration, then carry out the procedure on p. 13.

*Figure 6: The general seating position.*

❑ **Adjust the footstand to about seven inches in height and place it eight inches in front of the chair. Align the footstand with a point just inside the left front leg of the chair and a point midway between the two rear legs. Sit well forward on the chair, facing the same direction as the footstand. If necessary, move the footstand either forward or backward so that your lower leg is perpendicular to the floor. Sitting at an angle on the chair allows you to lower your right thigh (if necessary) without being impeded by the edge of the chair.**

❑ **Rest the guitar snugly against your left thigh. Rest the lower back rim of the guitar against your right thigh and the upper back rim against your chest.**

❑ **Hold the guitar in position by resting your right forearm on the front rim of the lower bout. Don't hook your elbow around the rim of the guitar — only your forearm should touch the guitar. Slide your forearm until your hand is over the edge of the soundhole nearest the bridge.† CAUTION: Don't raise your shoulder as you position your forearm on the guitar. Your right shoulder should remain level with your left shoulder.**

∞ ∞ ∞ ∞ ∞ ∞ ∞

The next step is to adjust your position so that it provides maximum advantage for both your hands. Adjusting your position, however, is an individual matter which depends on your overall physique: the length of your legs in relation to your torso, the width and slant of your shoulders, and your general build, whether heavy or slim. Thus, before you can begin to adjust your position, you'll need to consider the following information:

---

†To allow your forearm to slide freely on the guitar, wear either a long-sleeved shirt or a removable sleeve of stretch fabric over your right forearm (a sock with its foot section removed works well). This also protects the finish of the guitar from perspiration.

• **The Five Ways of Moving the Guitar:** This information provides you with a clear understanding of the various ways the position of the guitar can be adjusted.

• **The Right- and Left-Hand Position Checks:** This information provides you with basic aims as you begin adjusting your position.

## The Five Ways of Moving the Guitar

There are five ways in which the position of the guitar can be adjusted:

1) moving the guitar head forward or back
2) tilting the bottom of the guitar in or out on your left thigh
3) raising or lowering the guitar head
4) raising or lowering the entire guitar in relation to your torso
5) moving the entire guitar to the right or left in relation to your torso.

## The Right- and Left-Hand Position Checks

To position the guitar effectively and securely, you must find a playing position which provides free access to the strings with your right hand, and to the full range of the fingerboard with your left. The following position checks isolate the basic functions of each hand, allowing you to consider each hand separately.

*Figure 7A: Right-hand position check.*

### • *Right-Hand Position Check:*

❑ **Moving only from the elbow, swing your forearm up and down, carrying your hand across all six strings.**

## ·Left-Hand Position Check:

❏ **Place the first finger of your left hand across the 1st fret. Then move your left hand to place the tip of your fourth finger at the 19th fret.**

*Figure 7B: Left-hand position check.*

# Adjusting Your Position

Having been provided with the previous information, you're now ready to begin adjusting the general position of the guitar to your own individual physique. Although for now you won't be entirely comfortable in any position, you'll be least uncomfortable in a specific position, and you need to find that position.

> *• Your aim is to find an overall position in which your right hand can swing freely across the strings without being impeded by the rim of the guitar, and which gives your left hand the most comfortable access to the full range of the fingerboard.*

Using the procedure which follows, experiment with each of the five ways of moving the guitar separately, carrying out the right-hand check, then the left-hand check, and finally both checks together. Continually experiment within the positioning guidelines, trying different positions and footstand heights, to discover which adjustments are the most comfortable and advantageous.

*NOTICE:* In carrying out these adjustments, you'll often find that what's most comfortable for one hand will not be most comfortable for the other. Thus, you should aim to strike a compromise between the most comfortable position for each hand — finding a position which gives equal advantage to both hands.

Proceed as follows:

### 1) Moving the guitar head forward or back:

☐ **Right Hand:** Notice that this adjustment strongly affects the comfortable movement of your right forearm on the rim of the guitar. Your arm will be less impeded when the guitar head is positioned relatively far forward.

☐ **Left Hand:** Notice that positioning the guitar head far forward is awkward for your left hand — to place your finger across the 1st fret, you must strain your wrist past its limit of comfortable flexion. Your left hand moves most comfortably when the guitar head is positioned relatively well back.

☐ **The Compromise:** Place the guitar head only slightly forward. Although this isn't the most comfortable position for either hand, it provides equal advantage for both hands.

### 2) Tilting the bottom of the guitar in or out on your left thigh:

☐ **Right Hand:** Notice that this strongly affects the comfortable movement of your forearm on the rim of the guitar. Your arm will be less impeded when the guitar is tilted relatively far out on your thigh.

☐ **Left Hand:** Notice that tilting the guitar far out on your thigh is awkward for your left hand — to place your finger across the 1st fret, you must strain your wrist past its comfortable range of flexion. Your left hand moves most comfortably when the guitar is tilted inward on your thigh.

❏ **The Compromise:** The guitar should be held at a slight angle, with the bottom tilted slightly outward so that only the upper rim leans against your chest. Again, although this isn't the most comfortable position for either hand, it provides equal advantage for both hands.

## 3) Raising or lowering the guitar head:

❏ **Right Hand:** As long as you avoid extremes, this adjustment has little effect on right-hand comfort. Thus, you should concentrate mainly on the left-hand position check when making this adjustment.

❏ **Left Hand:** Notice that your left hand moves most comfortably when the guitar head is positioned relatively high. Avoid placing the guitar head too low — to place your finger across the 1st fret, you would need to twist your left forearm to the limit of its counterclockwise rotation.

## 4) Raising or lowering the entire guitar in relation to your torso:

❏ **Right Hand:** As long as you avoid extremes, this adjustment has little effect on right-hand comfort. Thus, you should concentrate mainly on the left-hand position check when making this adjustment.

❏ **Left Hand:** This adjustment strongly affects your ability to comfortably reach the higher frets. Your left hand moves most comfortably when the guitar is positioned relatively high in relation to your torso. To achieve this position, you may need to elevate the entire guitar by adjusting the footstand higher. You should be able to reach the 19th fret without having to dip your left shoulder.

## 5) Moving the entire guitar to the right or left in relation to your torso:

❑ **Right Hand:** As long as you avoid extremes, this adjustment has little effect on right-hand comfort. Thus, you should concentrate mainly on the left-hand position check when making this adjustment.

❑ **Left Hand:** Notice that this adjustment strongly affects your ability to comfortably reach the entire range of the fingerboard. Position the guitar far enough to the right so that you can reach the entire range of the fingerboard without twisting your torso out of comfortable alignment.

**CAUTION: Most students don't position the guitar far enough to the right to make the first few frets readily accessible.** The 1st fret is frequently used in guitar playing — the farther the guitar is positioned to the right, the more accessible is the 1st fret. Move the guitar until the soundhole is over or slightly to the right of the center of your torso.

Bear in mind that learning to position the guitar is a gradual process. If you're a beginner, every position will feel awkward at first. If you're an experienced guitarist, you may be so accustomed to a disadvantageous position that any alteration — even an advantageous one — will feel wrong. Thus, it may be some time before you finally arrive at a secure and comfortable position.

# An Alternative to Using the Footstand Alone

The position described in the preceding procedures is the traditional seating position for classic guitarists. Many guitarists, however, find that using the footstand alone results in awkward and uncomfortable positions. To position the guitar in correct relation to their torso, many find they must either raise their thigh in a sharply upward angle or compensate by hunching over the guitar. Further, to position the guitar far enough to the right, many students find they must either lean their torso to the left or point their left knee to the right. All these variations contradict the Principle of Muscular Alignment. Uncorrected, they introduce excess tension and often cause back pain.

One solution has proven comfortable and effective -- using an adjustable support with or without a footstand. By carefully adjusting the support, you can keep your left thigh in a comfortably horizontal position, and you can also move the guitar sufficiently to the right without disturbing the comfortable alignment of your body.

Using an adjustable support contributes so much to comfort and security that I no longer recommend positioning the guitar with the footstand alone. As you gain experience with positioning, you may wish to try this alternative to the traditional seating position.

*Figure 8: An adjustable support is used with or without a footstand.[†] (Notice that, in this figure, the guitar is positioned lower in relation to the torso than in Figure 6 [see p. 12]. This is because Figure 8 shows a guitarist of somewhat larger build than the guitarist in Figure 6. Generally, people of larger build will position the guitar lower in relation to their torso than people of smaller build.)*

---

[†]The adjustable support shown here is the *A-Frame,* which is available through Mel Bay Publications.
1-800-325-9518

## Summary

These positioning procedures will give you an acceptable position for beginning your training. Thus, you should concentrate for now on gaining coordination with right- and left-hand positioning and movements.

As you gradually gain coordination, however, you'll soon become more sensitive to your position — you'll begin to feel the advantages and disadvantages of subtle alterations. As you develop this sensitivity, you can begin to refine your position. Again, use the right- and left-hand position checks to carry out these refinements:

> • **Repeatedly try the right- and left-hand position checks separately and together.** Remember, what's most comfortable for one hand won't necessarily be most comfortable for the other.
>
> • **Learn to recognize excess tension.** Slightly alter one position, then another, striving to discover the position of least tension.
>
> • **As you become sensitive to excess tension, begin experimenting with extremes.** By discovering the disadvantages of obviously wrong positions, you'll become more sensitive to the advantages of slight adjustments.

*Above all, be patient.* You're building habits which strongly influence how much time you'll need to develop fine coordination of the hand muscles. Approach positioning with a spirit of experimentation, using the right- and left-hand positioning checks as your guides.

# Tone Production

When the guitar is well played, perhaps its most attractive characteristic is its tone. Tone production, however, is also one of the most problematic areas of guitar study. Poorly trained students produce a poor tone which is immediately evident during performance. Since your overall aim is to avoid anything which will hinder your effectiveness as a performer, you need to approach tone production with special care.

While a wide range of tone color is possible on the classic guitar, this range of tone color isn't your present concern. Rather, you should aim to develop an optimum basic tone which, through training, you can produce by habit. This basic tone will eventually be your point of departure for using the guitar's full range of color.

## Principles of Tone Production

Although everyone's basic tone varies, most guitarists agree on its more desirable qualities. Full-bodied, mellow, and warm are more desirable qualities — thin, hollow, and metallic are less desirable.

The quality and power of your tone depend on the following three principles:

> • *Tone Perception:* The tone you produce reflects the tone you perceive as desirable. You'll develop your perception by critically listening to yourself and others. You'll clarify and refine your tone perception as you progressively experiment with nail shape and the movements of your thumb and fingers.
>
> • *Nail Condition and Use:* Your tone depends on both the condition of your nails and how you use them.
>
> • *Touch and Movement:* Your tone depends on how your thumb or finger contacts the string, and on the direction and force of its movement when sounding the string:

> **a. The left tip and nail rim of the thumb or finger must be placed firmly against the string the instant prior to sounding the string.†**
>
> **b. Movement must be sufficiently firm to drive the string obliquely inward at the instant of the stroke. Thumb or finger movement must not be deflected by the string's tension.**

These principles function interdependently. You'll start with basic nail shapes which allow you to begin right-hand training. As you acquire habits of correct positioning and movement, you'll gradually refine the shape of your nails. Throughout this process, you'll be guided by the tone you perceive to be desirable. Your tone perception, however, will also be affected by the other two principles — as you refine your movement and nail shapes, you'll also refine your perception of a desirable tone.

## Tone Quality and Your Nails

You should begin using your nails as soon as they've grown to an adequate length for effective shaping. Sounding the strings with the nails requires different finger movements from those used when sounding the strings without the nails. By using your nails from the beginning of right-hand study, you'll avoid forming habits which must eventually be replaced.

A tone is produced at the precise instant the string departs from your nail. *How gradually or abruptly this departure occurs is a crucial element of tone production.* The departure of the string from your nail is affected by three main factors:

1) the movement of your thumb or finger
2) the shape of your nail
3) the position of your right hand — this is determined by the following:

†All left/right directions assume that you're viewing your hands in their playing positions. Thus, your right hand is viewed palm down — your left hand is viewed palm up.

a. the point at which your forearm crosses the guitar rim

b. the height of the guitar head

c. the height of the guitar in relation to your torso

d. the position of the guitar to the left or right of your torso

By applying the procedures in this book for movement and positioning, you'll contact the strings with the left side of your nails. The following illustrations show how the nail affects the resulting tone:

## *Nail Position and Shape which Cause a Gradual Departure of the String from the Nail.* These yield a mellow and full-bodied tone:

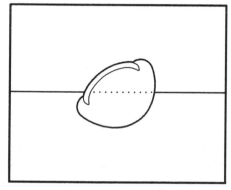 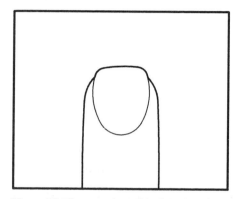

*Figure 9A: (Viewed from above, sighting down along the length of the finger toward the string.) The more perpendicular the nail rim is to the string, the more gradual is the departure of the string from the nail.[†]*

*Figure 9B: The more the nail is shaped to a level plane, the more gradual is the departure of the string from the nail.*

---

[†]This is clearly demonstrated by the *slice* or *side stroke*, attributed to Andres Segovia. Its practical application is limited, however, because it requires moving the entire hand sideways.

*Nail Position and Shape Which Cause an Abrupt Departure of the String from the Nail.* **These yield a bright and clear tone:**

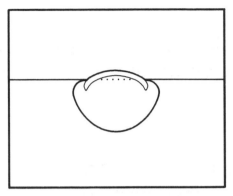

*Figure 10A: (Viewed from above.) The more parallel the nail rim is to the string, the more abrupt is the departure of the string from the nail.*

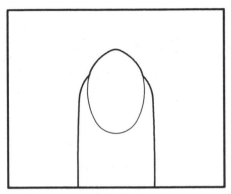

*Figure 10B: The more the nail is shaped to a point, the more abrupt is the departure of the string from the nail.*

While mellow and full-bodied tone qualities are generally desirable, they aren't the only important qualities of a basic tone. If overly dominant, they tend to obscure tonal clarity. Conversely, while thin and metallic tone qualities are generally less desirable, they do improve the clarity of tone. You should shape and use your nails to produce an appealing blend of these contrasting qualities. Of course, you can emphasize a darker or brighter tone according to your personal preference.

# Nail Contours and Suggested Shapings

Everyone's nails are different. Even your own nails may vary from finger to finger. Nails differ in curvature, thickness, texture, and the way they're set into the fingers. These differences, and even the different shapes and fullness of the fingertips, influence nail shaping. Because of these differences, it's impossible to give precise information about shaping individual nails. Nail shaping is a personal matter which requires careful experimentation and practice.

Nail shaping is strongly influenced by the contour of each individual nail. A *nail contour* refers to the profile of a nail. The following illustrations show general nail contours and their suggested shapings:

**The Thumb:**

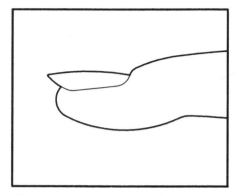

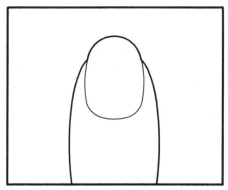

*Figure 11A: Relatively straight lengthwise contour.*

*Figure 11B: Suggested shaping.*

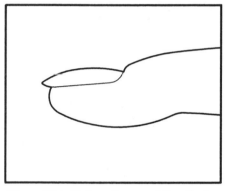

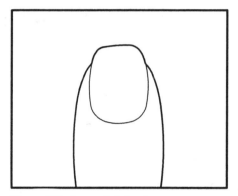

*Figure 12A: Extremely curved legnthwise contour.*

*Figure 12B: Suggested shaping.*

**The Fingers:**   **Moderately curved sideways and relatively straight lengthwise contour:**

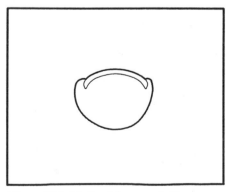

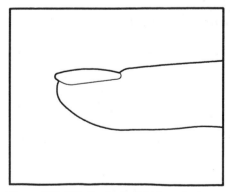

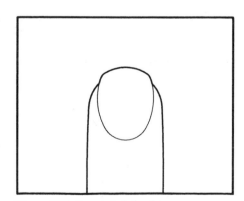

*Figure 13A: Moderately curved sideways.*

*Figure 13B: Relatively straight lengthwise.*

*Figure 13C: Suggested shaping.*

**Extremely curved sideways contour:**

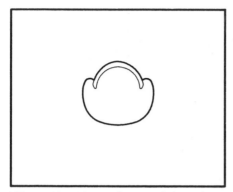

*Figure 14A: Unusually curved throughout entire profile.*

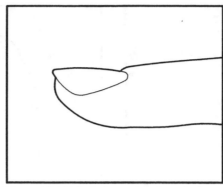

*Figure 14B: Relatively straight lengthwise.*

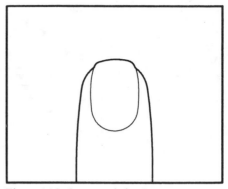

*Figure 14C: Suggested shaping.*

**Extremely curved lengthwise contour:**

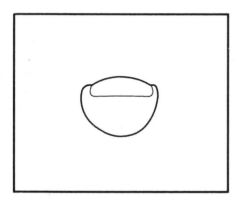

*Figure 15A: Moderately curved throughout entire profile.*

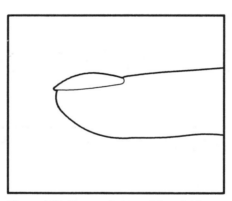

*Figure 15B: Extremely curved lengthwise.*

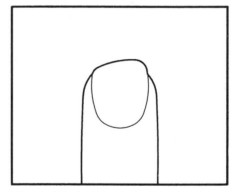

*Figure 15C: Suggested shaping.*

**The following variations are nail shapes (of the index, middle, and ring fingers) used by some well-known concert guitarists:**

*Figure 16A*

*Figure 16B*

General shaping of your nails should be done with a diamond-type file. To avoid a raspy sound, polish the rims of your nails to a glassy smoothness with extremely fine-grade sandpaper or a buffer board of similar grade. The final length of your nails should be determined by the tone you produce and by the ease of right-hand execution. Generally, however, you should try to keep your nails relatively short. Although short nails require more accurate placement, they're stronger and yield a more powerful tone.

## Summary

During the early stages of right-hand training, you should balance your concern about tone quality with the following considerations:

- Positioning your wrist and finger joints for maximum muscular advantage

- Firmly placing your tip and nail against the string

- Moving most effectively in sounding the string

You won't develop your best tone until you acquire secure habits in each of these areas. But be patient — these areas will be thoroughly explained in the following chapters on right-hand training. Carefully and consistently apply the right-hand training procedures in your study and practice. As you become more fluent, your tone will gradually improve.

As you begin refining your tone, remember the relationship between tone quality and nail departure. Since an extremely gradual departure of the nail from the string produces an indistinct tone, and an extremely abrupt departure produces a tone lacking body and mellowness, your aim is to strike a balance between these tone characteristics. Shape your nails so that they depart somewhat gradually from the string, giving you a rather mellow and full-bodied tone. But also remember that you want a distinct tone, with just enough of the abrupt departure characteristics to give your tone added brightness and clarity.

Bear in mind, however, that tone production isn't solely a right-hand consideration. Your tone is also affected by your left-hand fluency — a generally sloppy left-hand technique will detract from your overall tone. Thus, your tone is ultimately the sum of your proficiency with both hands.

# Beginning Right-Hand Training

## *Terms and Symbols*

Circled numbers, ①②③④⑤⑥, indicate strings.

In a musical score, the right-hand thumb and fingers are identified by the first letter of the Spanish terms *pulgar, indice, medio, anular,* and *chico.* (To avoid confusion, these letters will be underlined when they appear within text: p, i, m, a, c or P, I, M, A, C ).

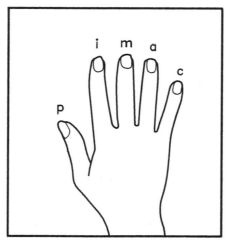

*Figure 17A: Right hand.*

The left-hand fingers are identified by Arabic numbers. The thumb requires no special identification.

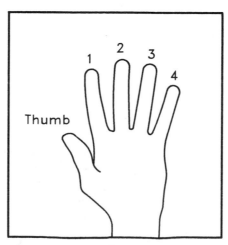

*Figure 17B: Left hand.*

The thumb and fingers each have three joints. The same names are used for the joints of both the right and left hands. **CAUTION:** Be sure to accurately distinguish between a joint and a segment. A joint is the point at which the thumb or finger bends — a segment is either the section between two joints, or (in the case of the tip segment) the section beyond the tip joint.

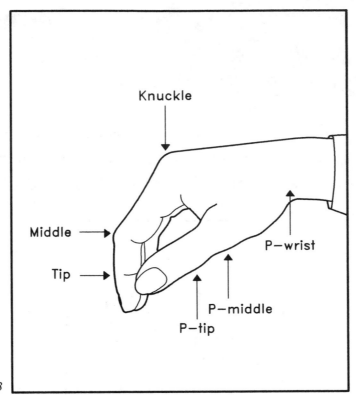

*Figure 18*

These directional terms are used for right-hand and wrist positioning.

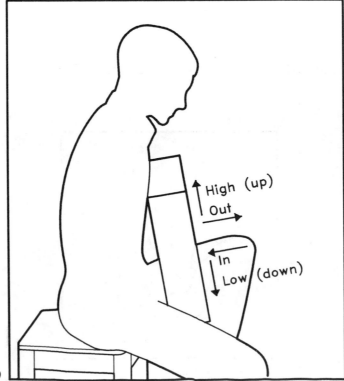

*Figure 19*

*The midway position* of a joint is the approximate midpoint between the comfortable limits of flexion and extension.

*The midrange movement* of a joint is approximately the middle two-quarters of the range between the comfortable limits of flexion and extension.

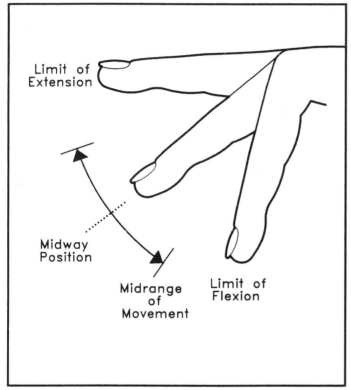

*Figure 20A: Positioning and range of movement at the knuckle joint.*

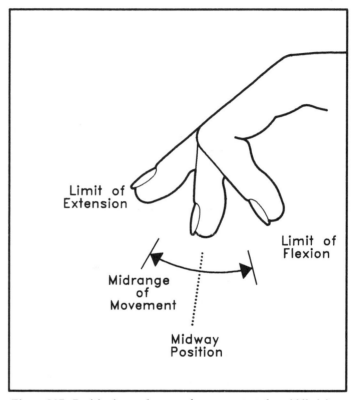

*Figure 20B: Positioning and range of movement at the middle joint.*

*Arch:* The result of flexion at your wrist joint.

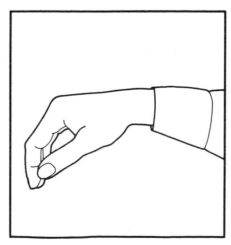

*Figure 21*

*Alignment:* The alignment of your wrist with your hand and forearm.

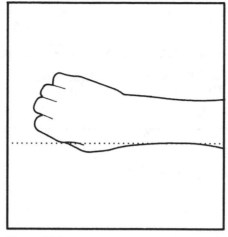

*Figure 22A*

*Deviation:* The sideways curvature of your wrist to either the right or left.

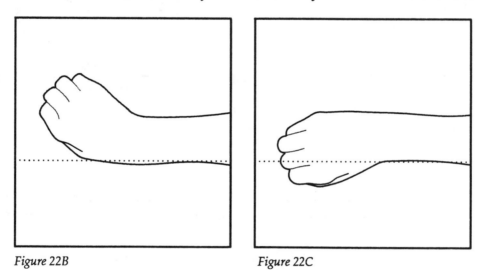

*Figure 22B*                     *Figure 22C*

*Tilt:* The orientation of your hand and fingers to the strings, resulting from the counterclockwise rotation of your forearm.

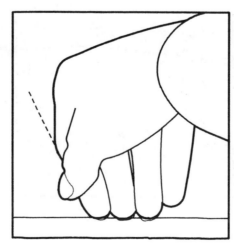

*Figure 23*

# *Right-Hand Positioning*

It's difficult to overemphasize the importance of right-hand positioning. It directly affects your development of coordination. An improper right-hand position will impede your progress as you begin learning thumb and finger movements.

Right-hand positioning involves two Principles of Efficient Muscle Function:

> **Muscular Alignment:** Muscles function most efficiently only when naturally aligned with their base and joint attachments.
>
> **Midrange Function of Joints:** Muscles function most efficiently only when the joints they control are operated within their midrange of movement.

Your aims are as follows:

> • To position your wrist according to the principle of muscular alignment
>
> • To arch your wrist and position the knuckle and middle joints of your fingers in their midway positions[†]
>
> • To establish the most effective tilt of your hand:
>
>     a. for optimum tone production
>     b. to equalize the length of your fingers
>     c. for the easiest, most direct extension and flexion of <u>p</u>

---

[†]Since the tip joints naturally position themselves along with the middle joints, they require no special consideration at this time.

Proceed as follows:

❏ **With your body and the guitar properly positioned, align the side of the i̲ knuckle with the side of your wrist and forearm. Notice that this aligns the m̲ knuckle with the center of your wrist and forearm, and the a̲ knuckle with its side of your wrist and forearm.**

❏ **Until you've acquired a feeling of this alignment, check it frequently with a mirror. Another helpful check is to place a pencil or ruler so that it lies flat against the side of your i̲ knuckle, wrist, and forearm.**

Now you need to determine the midway position of your wrist and knuckle joints:

❏ **Hold your right hand away from the guitar. Relax your finger joints as much as possible.**

❏ **Alternately flex and extend your wrist to its comfortable limits. *Notice that, when your wrist is fully flexed, your fingers become almost completely extended (see Figure 24A); and, when your wrist is fully extended, your fingers become almost completely flexed (see Figure 24B).***

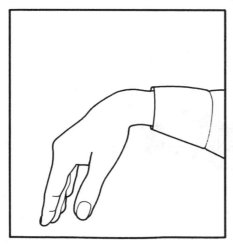

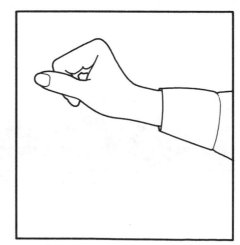

*Figure 24A*                     *Figure 24B*

❏ **Arch and hold your wrist in its midway position, so that your finger joints also assume their comfortable midway position (see Figure 24C).**

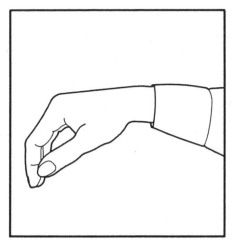

*Figure 24C*

❑ **With your wrist and fingers in their midway positions, place your forearm and hand in normal playing position (as you determined through the procedures on pp. 12 – 20.) As a point of reference, notice that the back of your hand is now approximately level with the plane of the strings.**

❑ **Tilt your hand to the left so that the tip and middle segments of a are approximately vertical to the plane of the soundboard.**

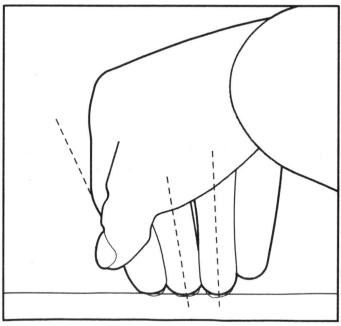

*Figure 25*

**The tip and middle segments of m will be tilted to the left, and those of i even more to the left. Again, a mirror is helpful until you've acquired a feeling of the proper tilt.**

Maintaining the proper position of your wrist and finger joints will be a demanding challenge when you begin the actual movement and training of p. You haven't gained sufficient coordination yet, and the resulting tension will tend to pull your wrist and finger joints into awkward positions. Thus, review the aims and procedures of positioning frequently, and make them habits during your daily study and practice. Strive to refine your position, achieving maximum advantage for your right-hand muscles.

## Rest-Stroke and Free-Stroke

The act of sounding a string is called a "stroke." There are two basic strokes used in guitar playing:

*Free-stroke:* (Spanish: *tirando*) Immediately after sounding a string, the finger or p swings freely above the adjacent string.

*Rest-stroke:* (Spanish: *apoyando*) Immediately after sounding a string, the finger or p comes to rest against the adjacent string.

Right-hand movement involves two Principles of Efficient Muscle Function:

> ***Uniform Direction of Joint Movement:*** Muscles function most efficiently only when adjacent joints of an individual finger or the thumb are either flexed together or extended together.
>
> ***Follow-Through:*** Muscles function most efficiently only when there is sufficient follow-through to avoid a build-up of counterproductive tension.

## The Prepared-Stroke

In the early stages of right-hand training, misdirected students often try to sound strings by moving p or their fingers in a continuous motion. Accurately moving p or the fingers in a continuous motion, however, requires an advanced level of skill. Students who try to begin with a continuous motion tend to miss strings and produce a poor tone. Thus, they begin to build habits of insecurity.

**Before you can confidently sound a string with a smooth and continuous motion, you must first acquire habits of accuracy and security. The prepared-stroke is the most efficient way to acquire these habits.**

*In the **prepared-stroke**, you pause to place the tip and nail against the string as precisely as possible.* As a right-hand training technique, the prepared-stroke offers the following advantages:

- It ensures accurate and firm placement of the tip and nail against the string.

- It yields an increased feeling of security.

- It speeds your progress toward being able to accurately and securely move p or your fingers in a continuous motion.

Because of these advantages, through most of your right-hand training you'll use the prepared-stroke when beginning new movement forms.

## Training P: The Prepared Free-Stroke

Starting your right-hand training with p has two advantages:

1) P affords ready access to the notes of the G-major triad: the open ②, ③, and ④ strings. By adding only a few notes with your left hand, you can produce remarkably appealing melodic and harmonic combinations.

2) The p free-stroke is initially easier to understand and execute than either the free-stroke or rest-stroke with the fingers. Thus, beginning with p provides the most immediate overall feeling of security for your right hand.

∽    ∽    ∽    ∽    ∽    ∽    ∽

Your priorities in training p are as follows:

> • To acquire a sense of security when placing the p tip and nail accurately and firmly against the string.
>
> • To move with sufficient firmness when sounding the string.

Before beginning, you should acquire a feeling of the basic movements used to sound a string with p. Without the guitar, carry out the following exercise:

❑ Establish the basic right-hand wrist position for playing the guitar (see pp. 33 – 36 ).

❑ Begin with p in its position of rest, with the tip joint slightly flexed and the tip segment resting lightly against the tip joint of i.

❑ Extend from the p-wrist joint to the comfortable limit of extension. Don't allow the tip joint to turn backward.

❑ Flex the p-tip and p-wrist joints together to bring the tip firmly back to its beginning position, slightly flexed against i. Emphasize movement from the p-wrist joint. Ideally, there should be no movement at the p-middle joint. Movement at the p-tip joint should be quite limited. Keep your hand and wrist steady.

❑ CAUTION:  Avoid circular motion of p. Circular motion is extremely complex and tends to cause counterproductive tension. Extend and flex as directly as possible — this is the least complex motion.

# *Sounding the Strings*

Your aims are as follows:

> • To extend precisely, placing your tip and nail firmly against the string in preparation for a firm movement when sounding the string.
>
> • To extend and flex from the p-wrist joint, with only slight movement at the p-tip joint.
>
> • To move to and from the string as directly as possible, avoiding the tension of a complex circular motion.
>
> • To follow through freely, coming to rest against i after sounding the string — this induces a release of tension in the muscles.

Proceed as follows:

❑ With your right wrist and finger joints in their midrange positions, place the tips of i and m on ① to stabilize your hand. Place the left tip and nail edge of p firmly against ③.

❑ Start the stroke by slightly flexing the p-tip joint; without hesitation sound the string by firmly flexing the p-wrist joint so that, when departing the nail, the string is deflected inward. *It should feel as though the tip and nail of p are digging into the string.* Follow through freely with p, bringing the tip segment to rest against i. (If you must begin training with a nail of inadequate length, use only as much of the tip of p as necessary to produce a full sound.)

❑ Extend p from its wrist joint. At the end of extension, a slight inward motion of p is needed to contact the string. *Don't exaggerate this extension and inward movement into a complex circular motion — keep extension as direct as possible.*

❑ **When re-sounding a vibrating string, be careful not to contact the string with the nail before contacting it with the tip. When both nail and tip are placed simultaneously, the tip dampens the objectionable noise which would result from contacting the vibrating string with the nail alone.**

❑ **Avoid the tendency to extend the p-tip joint before flexing it. Carefully flex or extend the joints together — never flex one while extending the other.**

❑ **If the p-middle joint tends to collapse, as it sometimes does if you're "double-jointed," keep this joint slightly flexed to brace it against the force of the stroke.**

❑ **Hold your hand and arm steady, and frequently check the tilt of your hand and the alignment and arch of your wrist. Until you can feel these important aspects of positioning without watching, you must establish them by sight.**

❑ *Work slowly and carefully!* **Until this movement form becomes a secure habit, emphasize firm placement and accurate movement rather than speed.**

∾ ∾ ∾ ∾ ∾ ∾ ∾

When you can sound ③ with acceptable accuracy and freedom, practice sounding ④. Then practice alternating between ③ and ④, always holding your hand steady. Then practice ②. Finally, practice the three strings in direct succession, one stroke for each string.

Once you can accurately perform the prepared free-stroke, you're ready to concentrate on the particular phase of this movement which requires special attention: the extension. Secure and fluent extension in preparation for the next stroke is the most challenging area of thumb and finger training. You can develop secure and fluent extension by practicing the prepared free-stroke in the following manner:

❑ **Begin by counting in twos at a slow tempo. A metronome setting of 52 (M.M. ♩ = 52) is about right.**

❑ **On the count of one, sound the string, bringing p to rest against i. On the count of two, extend precisely and place the tip and nail against the string. Sound the string again on the count of one. Practice without a break in counting. Hold p against i for the full count of one, and against the string for the full count of two. This will help you emphasize a more rapid and precise extension. When the movement feels secure, gradually increase the tempo.**

The prepared-stroke gives you a secure beginning in the training of p. With it, you'll form important habits of string contact and movement. Properly practiced, the prepared-stroke gives you a basis for a powerful, full-bodied tone and an overall sense of right-hand security.

# The Continuity-Stroke

The prepared-stroke, while essential for developing accuracy and security, has a relatively limited (though important) application in music. Since, in the prepared-stroke, you must pause to place the tip and nail against the string, you unavoidably dampen the string. Although this is useful in staccato playing, the demand for a smooth legato far exceeds that for staccato. Consequently, as soon as you feel secure with the prepared-stroke, you're ready to begin the continuity-stroke. In the *continuity-stroke,* your aim is to accurately place the tip and nail of p firmly against the string without a pause. The continuity-stroke is required not only for legato playing, but is also essential for your eventual development of speed.

Since we'll frequently refer to both the prepared and continuity-strokes, these concise definitions will be helpful:

• *The prepared-stroke is executed with a pause.*

• *The continuity-stroke is executed without a pause.*

Practice the continuity-stroke in the following manner:

❑ **As previously described, execute the p free-stroke at a slow tempo (M.M. ♩ = 52). However, rather than pausing to place your tip and nail, perform the stroke in a deliberate and continuous motion. Continue to emphasize direct extension and follow-through.**

❑ **BE CAUTIOUS! Students often tend to emphasize rapid movement at the expense of firm placement and tone. This is a serious error which becomes increasingly difficult to correct later.**

Bear in mind that, although the continuity-stroke is executed without a pause, it doesn't imply any lack of firm placement of the tip and nail against the string. If this movement feels insecure, practice the prepared-stroke again. Then alternately practice both — first the prepared-stroke, then the continuity-stroke.

## Summary

You need time and patience to develop secure habits of movement. There are no shortcuts, even for the most gifted students. Be certain you understand the principles involved. Begin with clear aims, and try to determine how the principles can best be applied to your aims. Find happiness in the marvelous process of learning this beautiful instrument. If you study and practice diligently, you can learn to play well.

You'll find musical examples for developing the p free-stroke in *Part Two*, pp. 14 – 20.

# Beginning Left-Hand Training

## *Before You Begin*

Although your left and right hands perform distinctly different movements when playing the guitar, both function according to the same muscular principles. Minimizing tension is as important to your left hand as it is to your right. Since you've previously focused on right-hand training, you may tend to favor your right hand when positioning the guitar. Uncorrected, this can cause counterproductive tension in your left hand.

To eliminate this possibility, you should again carry out the right- and left-hand position checks (pp. 14 – 15). Be alert to the following common errors:

> • Is the head of the guitar too low?
>
> • Is the head of the guitar too far forward?
>
> • Is the body of the guitar too low or too far to the left in relation to your torso?

Each of these errors can cause counterproductive left-hand tension. Experiment with both position checks until you find the position of maximum advantage for both hands.

# *Left-Hand Positioning*

In preparation for left-hand positioning, carefully study the following illustration:

*Figure 26*

Notice that the elbow hangs comfortably downward, and the wrist is slightly arched. The finger joints are in their powerful midrange positions.

Your aims of left-hand positioning are as follows:

> • **To maintain the natural alignment of your wrist.**
>
> • **To position your wrist and finger joints within their midrange of movement, and position your forearm within its midrange of rotation.**

Proceed as follows:

❑ **Based on your experiments with the left- and right-hand position checks, carefully place the guitar head at a height which allows your left forearm to function within its midrange of rotation.**

❑ **Compare your position to the following illustrations. With your left hand in playing position, your fourth-finger knuckle should be farthest from the side of the fingerboard, and your first-finger knuckle should be closest. Notice that each fingertip falls just behind its respective fret.**

| CORRECT LEFT-HAND POSITION | INCORRECT LEFT-HAND POSITION |
|---|---|

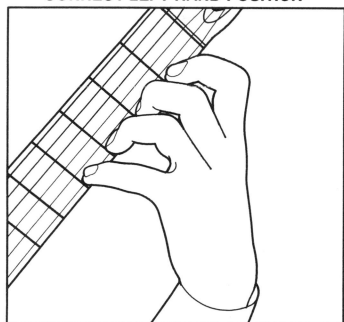
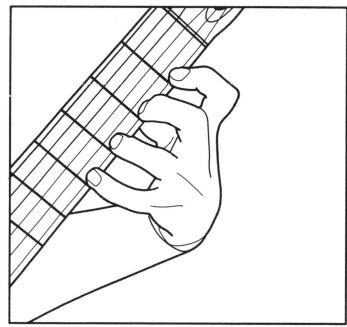

*Figure 27A: The most advantageous left-hand position. The fingers can extend lengthwise along the fingerboard with a minimum of tension.*

*Figure 27B: A poor left-hand position. The fingers must perform a tense lateral spread to reach their respective frets.*

## Left-Hand Movement

Before beginning, you need to consider the care of your left-hand nails. Keep them short enough so that they don't touch the fingerboard when you depress a string. Also, to present a neat appearance during performance, keep your nails carefully shaped, clean, and the cuticles gently pushed back.

You'll begin left-hand movement with one of the simplest movement forms in guitar playing: forming A (La) on ③ at the second fret with 2.[†]

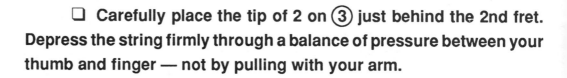

- **Your aim is to operate your finger joints within their mid-range of motion.**

Proceed as follows:

❑ **Carefully place the tip of 2 on ③ just behind the 2nd fret. Depress the string firmly through a balance of pressure between your thumb and finger — not by pulling with your arm.**

❑ **Alternately sound A (La) and G (So) slowly and evenly.**

❑ **For maximum leverage and balance, place the tip joint of your thumb against the back of the guitar neck at a point opposite your first two fingers.** *CAUTION: Apply the minimum pressure needed to produce a clear tone.* **Carefully avoid unnecessary tension in your left hand and forearm.**

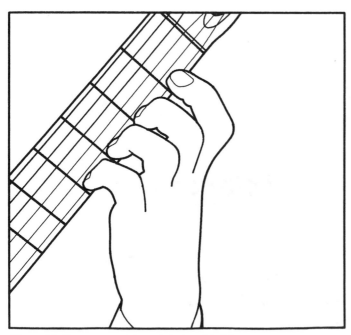

❑ **Avoid drawing your fingers back (hyperextending) at the knuckles, as shown in Figure 28. With your fingers correctly positioned in their midrange, movement for depressing the strings occurs mainly at the knuckles.**

❑ **When your fingers aren't contacting the strings, keep the joints well within midrange so that your fingertips remain comfortably suspended over the strings.**

*Figure 28: Incorrect position of the knuckle joints.*

[†]Since solfege will become an essential part of your training, musical notes will often be identified by both letter name and solfege syllable. You'll find an introduction and explanation of solfege syllables in *Part Two*, p. 209.

Cultivate a sensitivity to counterproductive tension. Experiment by slightly altering the sideways position of your elbow, the rotation of your forearm, and the arch of your wrist. Practice freely altering these positions to determine the position of greatest strength and ease for your left-hand fingers.

## Movement by Touch: Applying Aim-Directed Movement (ADM)

At first you'll need to watch the fingerboard as you execute left-hand movements — this is the quickest and easiest way to ensure the accurate placement of your fingers. To read music proficiently, however, you must learn to accurately place your fingers by touch rather than sight. You should begin this process as soon as you've gained confidence in executing left-hand movements by sight.

In doing this, you're beginning to apply ADM to left-hand movement. *When applied to the left hand, ADM is the process of knowing where to move your fingers on the fingerboard before actually moving them.*

Proceed as follows, beginning with A (La) on ③ at the 2nd fret with 2:

❑ **Count slowly and evenly in twos. While watching the fingerboard, alternately sound the open G (So) and A (La) as before. As you repeat these movements, look away from the fingerboard. Try to maintain the repeated accurate placement of your finger.**

❑ **Be sensitive to error. If, as you're looking away from the fingerboard, you feel your finger starting to creep away from the fret, stop and reestablish the fret location by sight.**

❑ **Maintain the natural alignment of your wrist and finger joints, and keep your forearm, wrist, and finger joints within their midrange positions. As you gain security, look away from the fingerboard for increasingly longer intervals. Continue this procedure until you can accurately and confidently place your finger by touch.**

❑ **Practice until you can clearly visualize left-hand movements away from the guitar — seeing them in your mind's eye as though you're actually executing them on the fingerboard.**

When you can confidently play A (La), repeat this procedure, alternating between the open B (Ti) and C (Do) on ② at the 1st fret with 1. Then alternate between C (Do) and D (Re) at the 3rd fret with 3 (or 4).

You'll find musical examples for practicing left-hand movement in *Part Two*, pp. 22 – 35.

# Training the Right-Hand Fingers

The following illustrations show the movements for rest-stroke and free-stroke with the fingers:

**REST-STROKE**

**FREE-STROKE**

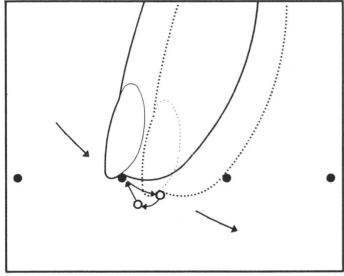 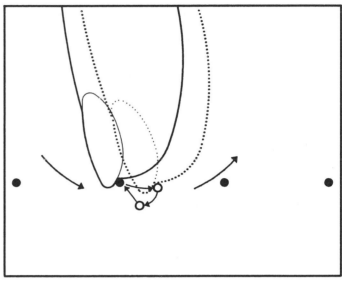

*Figure 29A*  *Figure 29B*

In training your right-hand fingers, you should concentrate on discovering the most effective hand positions and finger movements.[†] This will enable you to develop the coordination essential for accuracy and a desirable tone.

## *Training the Inactive Fingers*

In right-hand movement forms, an *inactive finger* is any finger which isn't involved in the process of either sounding or preparing to sound a string. Depending on how it's trained, an inactive finger can either assist or severely impede the movement of an adjacent active finger. Thus, during any right-hand movement form, inactive fingers should always be considered:

---

[†]Before beginning, make sure your nails are adequately shaped for right-hand finger training. (See "Nail Contours and Suggested Shapings," pp. 24 – 27.)

> • *An inactive finger should always move with an adjacent active finger.* As it moves, the inactive finger should remain slightly more flexed than the finger with which it's moving.
>
> • *Never allow an inactive finger to remain rigidly flexed or extended.* This would impede the movement of the active fingers.

Whether a finger is active or inactive depends on the movement form you're executing. Thus, each new right-hand movement form introduced in this book will be accompanied by information on movement of inactive fingers.

# The Prepared Rest-Stroke

In training p, you began with the free-stroke. In the early stages of finger-movement training, however, the rest-stroke will give you a stronger feeling of right-hand stability. Thus, you'll begin with the rest-stroke.

Your aims for rest-stroke positioning and movement are as follows:

> • To position your knuckle and middle joints so that, at the instant of sounding the string, they are in approximate midway positions.
>
> • To use the prepared-stroke, pausing to place your tip and nail firmly against the string.
>
> • To flex both the knuckle and middle joints to sound the string, bringing your finger to rest securely against the lower adjacent string.[†]

---

[†]Used with reference to strings, the terms *higher* and *lower* always refer to pitch. For example, to describe the strings adjacent to ③, ② is the higher adjacent string, and ④ is the lower adjacent string. **CAUTION:** Do not confuse these terms with the directional terms for positioning your right hand (see Figure 19, p. 30).

Proceed as follows:

❑ **With your body and the guitar in proper position, place your wrist, hand, and finger joints in the position described on pp. 34 – 35.**

❑ **Without changing the midway position of the finger joints and wrist, position your hand over the strings. Place the left tip of i̱ (very close to the nail) firmly against ①. (If your nails aren't yet of adequate length, use only as much of the fingertip as needed to produce a full sound.)**

❑ **Keep the middle (and tip) joints of m̱, a̱, and c̱ slightly flexed. To stabilize your hand, place the tip of p̱ against either ④ or ⑤. Your wrist, hand, and fingers should now be in the position shown in Figure 30:**

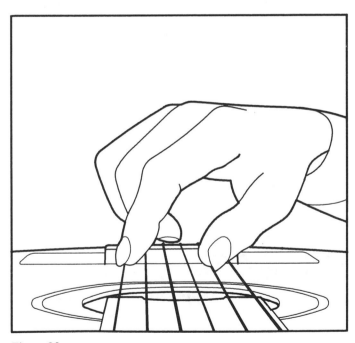

*Figure 30*

❑ **While holding your hand steady, sound ① with i̱ by flexing both the knuckle and middle joints. Keep the tip joint as firm as necessary to produce a good tone. Your finger should come to rest firmly against ②. *As inactive fingers, m̱–a̱–c̱ should be kept flexed a little past midway and slightly moving with i̱.***

❑ **With your hand properly aligned with your forearm, the slanted left edge of the nail will contact and cross the string diagonally.**

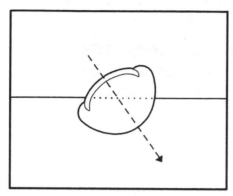

*Figure 31 (Viewed from above.)*

❑ **Extend i̱ back to ① and prepare another stroke. Limit extension to the amount needed to reach the string. (Notice that middle joint extension must be briefly delayed until a slight extension of the knuckle allows your fingertip to clear the vibrating string.)**

∞    ∞    ∞    ∞    ∞    ∞    ∞

As in training p̱, secure and fluent extension of i̱ requires special attention. You need to cultivate smooth and well-defined movements, allowing a sufficient pause to prepare each stroke.

Practice the prepared rest-stroke by counting evenly in twos — sound the string on the count of one; extend and prepare another stroke on the count of two. Make sure you move with the firmness needed to obtain a clear and full-bodied tone.

While slowly repeating the prepared rest-stroke, listen closely to your tone. If it's harsh, the cause may be one or any combination of the following:

> • **Your nail is too long.**
>
> • **Your nail is too pointed.**

> • **Your left nail rim isn't contacting the string diagonally enough (see Figure 31, p. 52).**
>
> • **You're not preparing and executing the stroke firmly enough.**

If your nail tends to catch on the string, or your finger tends to slip across and sound the adjacent string, begin the stroke with the middle joint slightly more extended.

When you gain reasonable control with i̲, begin training m̲ on ①:

❑ **Since m̲ is a longer finger, you must position your hand slightly higher to achieve optimum midway position of m̲'s middle joint. I̲, a̲, and c̲ should remain slightly flexed and move with each stroke of m̲.** *Never allow a̲ and c̲ to become rigidly extended when flexing m̲.*

❑ **In the manner previously described, practice the prepared rest-stroke with a̲. Keep c̲ slightly more flexed and moving with a̲.** *A and c̲ should always move together.*

Also practice sounding ② and ③; first with i̲, then with m̲, and then with a̲. To maintain the midway position of the finger joints, you'll need to reposition your hand over the strings; move only at the elbow joint — *do not reach with the fingers or change the position of your wrist.*

## The Continuity Rest-Stroke

When the prepared rest-stroke feels secure, you should begin practicing the continuity rest-stroke. Continue to carry out the same firm tip and nail placement. As always, don't rush this procedure — if your tone or accuracy deteriorates when you attempt the continuity-stroke, you need more practice with the prepared-stroke.

You'll find musical examples for developing the rest-stroke with your fingers in *Part Two,* pp. 36 – 40.

# Alternation of a Finger Rest-Stroke and _P_ Free-Stroke

You'll find this stage of technical development to be particularly rewarding. Now you can begin playing solo pieces consisting of a melody and a bass.

Alternation of a finger and p means you no longer have the steadying support of p on a lower string while playing a finger rest-stroke, nor the support of a finger on a higher string while playing a p free-stroke. This lack of support may cause a noticeable increase in tension throughout your right arm and shoulder. Students often attempt to minimize this tension by trying consciously to relax their arm and shoulder muscles. The reason for this tension, however, is a lack of coordination — you haven't yet acquired the essential habits for alternating the fingers and p. Thus, your most productive procedure is to concentrate on adequately training p and the fingers. With thoughtful practice, your initial feelings of excess tension and insecurity will soon be replaced with relaxation and stability.

Proceed as follows:

❑ **Without resting p on a string, practice the prepared rest-stroke, first with i, then m, and then a. Keep p in a relaxed, slightly flexed position and resting against i. _Move only your fingers; keep your hand steady._**

❑ **Now begin slowly alternating i and p, with i sounding ② and p sounding ⑤. Use prepared-strokes for both i and p. As i sounds its string, extend and place p; as p sounds its string, extend and place i.**

❑ **In the same manner, practice sounding ① with m and ⑤ with p; then ② with i and ⑥ with p. Check often to ensure that a and c are flexed and moving with m. Never allow c to assume a rigidly extended position past a, as is its tendency. _A and c should always function as a unit, flexing or extending together._**

When you can confidently produce a satisfactory tone with prepared-strokes, practice the same combinations of strings and fingers with continuity-strokes.

_Although the musical examples on pp. 44 – 50 of Part Two don't require continuous alternation of p and a finger, when alternation is required, be sure to extend p as your finger sounds its string and extend your finger as p sounds its string._

# Beginning Free-Stroke with Your Fingers

## *Before You Begin*

Unlike rest-stroke, during free-stroke your finger doesn't come to rest against the lower adjacent string. Rather, it follows through freely above the lower adjacent string. Thus, in the early stages of finger training, the free-stroke will feel less secure than the rest-stroke. But with the security you've acquired through the rest-stroke, you'll find that the free-stroke will also become a secure and powerful stroke.

Before you actually begin sounding strings with this stroke, you should acquire a general idea of the free-stroke movement away from the guitar. Using the nails of $\underline{i}$ and $\underline{m}$, you'll find that it's quite similar to a scratching motion. Proceed as follows:

❑ **Assume the now-familiar midway position of your right wrist and knuckle joints. Place the middle joints well on the flexion side of midrange and place the tips of $\underline{i}$ and $\underline{m}$ against the back of your left hand.**

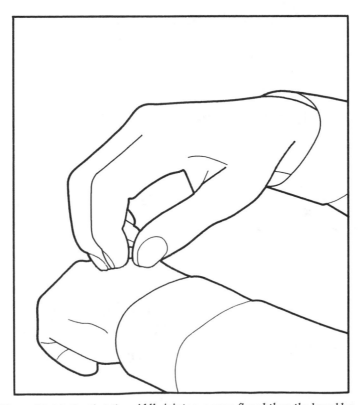

*Figure 32: Notice that the middle joints are more flexed than the knuckles.*

❑ Moving **i** and **m** together in the same direction, gently scratch the back of your left hand. **I** and **m** should touch the back of your left hand only during flexion. **I** should lightly brush against **p**.

❑ Notice that much more movement occurs at the middle joints than at the knuckles. The tip joints automatically extend and flex along with the middle joints.

❑ Maintain your wrist in the properly arched and aligned position during finger movement.

Review this exercise frequently as you begin developing the free-stroke.

# Free-Stroke Considerations

The following are important considerations as you begin sounding strings with the free-stroke:

• The arch and alignment of your wrist and the tilt of your hand are identical for both rest-stroke and free-stroke.

• The knuckle joint should remain in the same position for both rest-stroke and free-stroke, arriving at its midway position the instant your finger contacts the string.

• At the instant your finger contacts the string, the angle of the middle joint determines whether the stroke will be a rest-stroke or a free-stroke.

If you attempt free-stroke with the middle joint insufficiently flexed, the only way to clear the adjacent lower string is to extend the knuckle and simultaneously flex the middle joint — this contradicts the Uniform Direction of Joint Movement Principle and thus reduces the power of the stroke (see Figures 33A and 33B).

**CORRECT FREE-STROKE POSITION**     **INCORRECT FREE-STROKE POSITION**

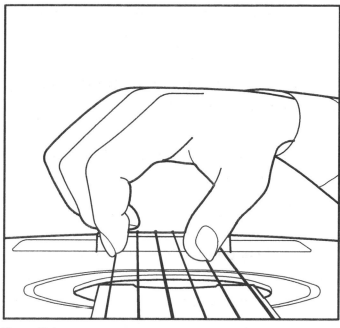

*Figure 33A*

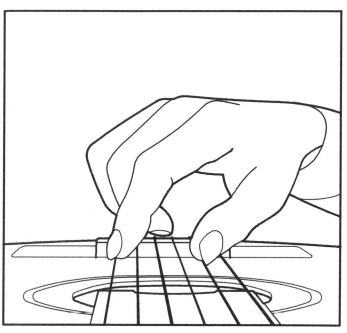

*Figure 33B*

Your aims for developing free-stroke with your fingers are as follows:

• To keep the middle joints sufficiently flexed and the tip joints sufficiently firm for the fingers to clear the lower adjacent strings.

• To move and follow through mainly from the middle joints, with a slight follow-through at the knuckles.

# <u>I</u>–<u>M</u> Free-Stroke†

Begin by sounding ③ and ② simultaneously with <u>i</u>–<u>m</u> as follows:

❏ **Position your hand and finger joints as though aiming to sound ① with <u>i</u> rest-stroke. Place <u>p</u> against ⑤ to steady your hand.**

❏ **While maintaining your hand position, flex the middle joints of <u>m</u> and <u>i</u> into prepared-stroke positions against ② and ③ respectively. Keep <u>a</u> and <u>c</u> somewhat more flexed than <u>m</u> and <u>i</u>.**

❏ **Flex firmly at the middle and knuckle joints to sound ② and ③. Flex more from the middle joints than from the knuckles, and keep the tip joints of both fingers quite firm. Follow through to the comfortable limit of <u>i</u>–<u>m</u> flexion. For now, exaggerate the follow-through of <u>a</u> and <u>c</u>, with <u>c</u> perhaps curling to touch your palm — this will help you establish the habit of flexing <u>c</u> along with <u>a</u>.**

❏ **Extend your fingers as directly as possible to prepare the next stroke. Avoid a complex circular motion.**

∞ ∞ ∞ ∞ ∞ ∞ ∞

Listen to your tone. If it's either harsh or weak, the cause may be any combination of those previously given for rest-stroke (pp. 52 – 53). When you've gained reasonable control and security in sounding ② and ③, practice sounding ① and ② simultaneously with <u>i</u>–<u>m</u>. To maintain the same finger joint positions, lower your hand the distance of one string. Remember to move only at the elbow (see p. 53).

Although it's essential that you begin with the prepared-stroke, bear in mind that your eventual goal is to develop the continuity-stroke.

You'll find musical examples for beginning the free-stroke with your fingers in *Part Two*, pp. 51 – 53.

---

†A hyphen between right-hand symbols indicates that those fingers are moved simultaneously in the same direction.

# *Tip Joint Considerations*

At the instant your finger sounds a string, you may find that the resistance of the string tends to push the tip joint into a hyperextended position.[†] You should learn to avoid this. *Always maintain enough firmness in the tip joint to avoid its being displaced by the resistance of the string.*

Maintaining sufficient firmness in the tip joint offers the following advantages:

> • It gives you a more secure feeling of digging into the string.
>
> • It helps the finger to clear the adjacent lower string.
>
> • It improves the brightness and clarity of your tone.
>
> • As your right-hand coordination improves, it gives you finer control of tone color.

There are certain situations in which guitarists allow the tip joint to hyperextend when sounding a string. But this is an advanced technique, and its application is limited. As a basic technique, don't allow the tip joint to hyperextend.

# *I–M and P Alternation*

Alternation of your fingers with p requires an advanced level of coordination. Neither p nor the fingers can provide stability for your hand by resting or coming to rest against a string. Before beginning i–m and p alternation, make sure you can securely perform the following movements:

• I–m free-stroke, with p lightly resting against the side of i

• P free-stroke with your fingers flexed enough to avoid touching the strings

[†]*Hyperextended* means that the tip segment is extended past its point of alignment with the middle segment.

Your right hand should remain relatively steady — you can minimize right-hand movement by emphasizing movement at the middle joints of i–m. When you can execute these movements with reasonable accuracy and fluency, proceed with alternation of i–m and p.

Your aims for developing i–m and p alternation are as follows:

> • **To extend and prepare p as you sound the strings with i–m, and to extend i–m as you sound the string with p.**
>
> • **To keep your right hand (and arm) properly positioned and steady as you sound the strings.**

Using prepared-strokes, proceed as follows:

> ❑ **Carefully position i on ③ and m on ②. P should rest lightly against i.**
>
> ❑ **Sound ③ – ② while preparing p on ⑤; then sound ⑤ while preparing i–m on ③ – ②.**

As you practice this movement form, remember the following:

> • **Move your fingers and p simultaneously, flexing one while extending the other. Any delay between these motions will impede your development of fluency and speed.**
>
> • **Emphasize movement at the middle joint of your fingers and the p-wrist joint.**
>
> • **For muscular freedom, follow through sufficiently with both your fingers and p, with p coming to rest against i.**

Bear in mind that your eventual goal is the smooth legato of the continuity-stroke. While the prepared-stroke is essential in the beginning, as you gain security with the movement, you should gradually lessen the pause needed to place your tip and nail firmly against the string.

You'll find musical examples for developing i–m and p alternation in *Part Two*, p. 54 and pp. 64 – 65.

# I–M–A Free-Stroke

The most effective way to begin training a is with the i–m–a free-stroke. A naturally tends to move with m, so i–m–a is simply a matter of adding a to your already secure i–m movement.

In any movement form involving a, always position a for maximum leverage. In free-stroke, the middle joint of a should be flexed in its powerful midrange position when a contacts the string:

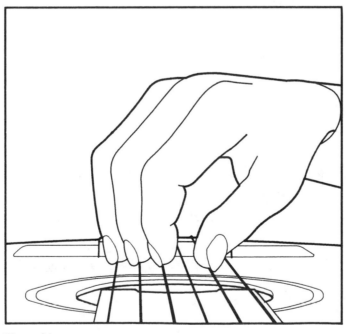

*Figure 34*

To allow a to assume its optimum position, m and i must operate in the flexion side of their midranges.

Since the note sounded by a̱ is usually the melody, this note should predominate. If you listen carefully, however, you'll notice the sounds produced by i̱ and m̱ tend to overpower the sound produced by a̱. You can correct this tendency by practicing with prepared-strokes and emphasizing the firm placement and follow-through of a̱.

Practice the i̱–m̱–a̱ exercises in *Part Two*, p. 69 as follows:

❑ **Steady your right hand by placing p̱ on a lower string ( ⑤ or ⑥ ).**

❑ **Emphasize a more pronounced follow-through with a̱ than with the other fingers. C̱ should be slightly flexed and moving with a̱.**

Since a̱ isn't as naturally coordinated as either i̱ or m̱, it responds more slowly to practice. To gain fluency with i̱–m̱–a̱, you'll need considerable practice with the prepared-stroke, giving special attention to a̱. Avoid the tendency to keep the knuckles too flexed — emphasize flexion and follow-through at the middle joints.

As you gain security, begin practicing i̱–m̱–a̱ without supporting your hand with p̱. P̱ should remain in its inactive position, with its tip lightly resting against i̱.

# I̱–M̱–A̱ and P̱ Alternation

This movement form is very similar to p̱ and i̱–m̱ alternation. Thus, you should practice it in a similar manner. Always try to keep the proper balance of sound between the fingers — train a̱ to move firmly enough for its sound to predominate.

You'll find musical examples for this movement form in *Part Two*, p. 70.

# Sympathetic Movement

When you flex or extend one finger, the adjacent finger tends to move in the same direction. This is called *sympathetic movement,* and it's extremely useful in playing the guitar. In sympathetic movement, adjacent fingers can move in the same direction either simultaneously or successively. Simultaneous movement and successive movement are very similar — only the timing between the two is different.

Sympathetic flexion or extension of your fingers is a further instance of the Uniform Direction of Joint Movement Principle. This principle applies not only to joints of an individual finger, but also to the same joints of adjacent fingers.

In guitar playing, sympathetic movement requires a high degree of timing and control. When effectively developed, sympathetic movement is a powerful aid for the rapid and continuous sounding of successive strings (arpeggios, for example). For now, however, you should concentrate on gaining coordination and control. Defer considerations of speed until you've developed secure habits of movement through the prepared-stroke — this will give you a secure basis for developing fluency and speed.

## *P, I, M*[†]

Your aims in establishing the p, i, m movement form are as follows:

- To sound ⑤, ③, and ② in succession with p, i, m (prepared free-strokes).

- To achieve controlled timing of the sympathetic movement between i and m.

---

[†]A comma between right-hand symbols indicates successive movement of those fingers.

Proceed as follows:

❑ **Place p against ⑤ with i–m(a–c) flexed above the strings.**

❑ **Sound ⑤ with p while extending and preparing i–m on③– ②.**

❑ **Sound③with i, flexing mainly at the middle joint. This naturally exerts a pull on m which increases as i follows through; flex m sympathetically with i to sound ② while simultaneously extending and preparing p. Notice that i always remains more flexed than m during both flexion and extension.**

> **Stated concisely, the p, i, m movements are as follows:**
>
> **a) As p sounds its string and follows through, the fingers extend and prepare.**
>
> **b) i sounds its string and begins following through.**
>
> **c) As m(a–c) moves sympathetically with i to sound its string, p extends and prepares for its next stroke.**

When you can carry out these movements with reasonable accuracy, practice them while slowly and evenly counting in threes (1, 2, 3; 1, 2, 3; etc.); give one count each for p, i, and m. Practice at a tempo which allows you to maintain a smooth and accurate flow of movement.

∾    ∾    ∾    ∾    ∾    ∾    ∾

The musical disadvantage of the prepared-stroke is obvious during the p, i, m movement form. In arpeggios, the prepared-stroke dampens tones which should be sustained until the harmony changes. Thus, you eventually want to develop secure and powerful continuity-strokes with the sympathetic movement forms. *But don't try to rush your development!* Learning sympathetic movement forms takes time. You should begin practicing continuity-strokes only when you've acquired sufficient coordination and security with prepared-strokes.

When you're ready to begin practicing with continuity-strokes, continue to extend your fingers simultaneously, but extend m approximately 3/8" from its string. Then, as you sound the string with i and follow through, m will be pulled firmly against its string, will sound the string, and will follow through in full sympathetic movement.

Notice that, when you play an arpeggio using continuity-strokes, the fingers are placed successively through sympathetic movement. This contrasts with the prepared-stroke, where your fingers are placed against the strings simultaneously. Bear in mind that the continuity-stroke requires the same firm placement of your tip and nail against the string as the prepared-stroke.

Proceed slowly and patiently. Let tone quality and a sense of security dictate your practice tempo. With careful practice, you'll soon develop rapid and accurate continuity-strokes with the p, i, m movement form.

You'll find musical examples for p, i, m in *Part Two*, pp. 71 – 75.

# P, I, M–A

P, i, m–a is the p, i, m movement form with a included. This allows you to continue your training of a in the easiest and quickest way possible.

Practice p, i, m–a in a manner similar to p, i, m. Bear in mind the following as you practice:

> • Position a for maximum leverage — i and m will function in more flexed positions.
>
> • Continually check the tilt of your hand — don't allow your hand to drift out of correct position.
>
> • Prepare p as a–m flex.
>
> • Emphasize the stroke of a.

You'll find exercises for developing p, i, m–a in *Part Two*, p. 76.

# P, I–M, A

In this movement form, the sympathetic movement occurs between <u>m</u> and <u>a</u>. Since there's less independence between <u>m</u> and <u>a</u> than between <u>i</u> and <u>m</u>, the <u>p</u>, <u>i</u>–<u>m</u>, <u>a</u> movement form is more challenging than <u>p</u>, <u>i</u>, <u>m</u>–<u>a</u>. To develop the timing of the sympathetic movement between <u>m</u> and <u>a</u>, you'll need to practice carefully and patiently.

*Students often neglect the preparation of <u>p</u> — make sure you prepare <u>p</u> as <u>a</u> flexes.*

You'll find exercises for developing <u>p</u>, <u>i</u>–<u>m</u>, <u>a</u> in *Part Two*, p. 76.

# Alternation

The primary purpose of finger alternation is speed of execution. When well developed, alternation allows you to sound notes on one or more strings in extremely rapid succession. To develop speed, however, you must first gain sufficient coordination and control of the alternation movement.

Although adjacent fingers tend either to flex together or extend together, *alternation* requires that they move in opposite directions — one finger simultaneously extending as the other flexes. To carry out this opposed movement with accuracy, fluency, and power, you must develop an entirely new level of coordination.

You can accelerate your development by supplementing your practice with hand exercises away from the guitar. These exercises are explained in "Conditioning and Coordination Exercises for Your Hands," p. 106. If you aren't already doing these exercises, you should start immediately and make them part of your daily routine.

Before you begin, you should acquire an understanding of the basic alternation movements. Proceed as follows, *without the guitar:*

❏ **Assume the familiar midway position of your wrist and fingers. P should be in its position of rest, lightly touching i.**

❏ **Alternately flex and extend i and m(a–c). Remember, i and m must move simultaneously in opposite directions. Move mainly at the middle joints, flexing to the comfortable limit of flexion and extending slightly past the midrange position. Avoid opposed movement between the knuckle and middle joints — your knuckles should slightly flex or extend with the middle joints.**

❏ **When you can do this evenly at moderate tempo, proceed in a similar manner to alternate m with a. I should move with m, and c should move with a.**

❏ **Carefully maintain the midway position of your wrist. During the early stages of alternation development, tension from lack of coordination often causes your wrist to extend out of its midway position.**

# *Beginning Free-Stroke Alternation: <u>P</u>, <u>I</u>, <u>M</u>, <u>I</u>*

When you began training individual fingers, you learned that the rest-stroke yielded a quicker feeling of security for your right hand (p. 50). During your early development this is true — considerations of right-hand stability make the rest-stroke easier and more secure. By now, however, you should be reasonably secure with both the rest-stroke and free-stroke. The considerations of right-hand stability which initially made the rest-stroke easier no longer apply. Thus, you'll begin alternation training with the free-stroke.

Because of the different reaches of <u>i</u> and <u>m</u>, alternation is best begun on adjacent strings by adding one opposed movement with <u>i</u> to the already secure <u>p, i, m</u> figure. This results in the <u>p, i, m, i</u> movement form. <u>P, i, m, i</u> consists of one opposed movement and one sympathetic movement of the fingers:

a) After sounding its string, <u>i</u> extends as <u>m</u> flexes — this is the opposed movement.

b) As <u>m</u> begins its follow-through and <u>i</u> sounds its string the second time, <u>i</u> flexes with <u>m</u> — this is the sympathetic movement.

Your aims in beginning free-stroke alternation are as follows:

> • To ensure that, at the instant <u>i</u> moves in one direction, <u>m</u> moves in the other.
>
> • To emphasize security rather than speed.

Proceed as follows:

❑ Begin with the familiar <u>p, i, m</u> movement sounding ⑤, ③, ②, except now extend and prepare <u>i</u> on ③ as <u>m</u> flexes to sound ②.

❑ While following through with <u>m</u>, again sound ③ with <u>i</u> and simultaneously extend and place <u>p</u> against ⑤. <u>l–m</u> (and <u>a–c</u>) should remain flexed.

❑ **While sounding ⑤ with p, lead with m(a–c) to extend and place i–m on their respective strings. This begins another cycle of p, i, m, i.**

∾   ∾   ∾   ∾   ∾   ∾   ∾

If, during flexion you touch an adjacent lower string (most often this occurs with i), one of the following may be the cause:

> • **You're not beginning the movement with the middle joint (and perhaps the tip joint) sufficiently flexed.**
>
> • **You're not sufficiently flexing the middle joint.**
>
> • **You're not keeping the tip joint sufficiently firm at the instant of the stroke.**

When you can execute p, i, m, i with reasonable accuracy, practice slowly and evenly while counting "1, &, 2, &." Practice at a tempo which allows you to maintain a smooth and accurate flow of movement.

Try to produce a full-bodied, clear, and somewhat mellow tone. If your tone is thin or too bright, flex with less firmness at the tip joint. If your tone is weak and unclear, flex with more firmness at the tip joint. Remember, you must apply sufficient power to deflect the string inward with the nail rim.

Experiment with all aspects of tone production to determine your best nail shape, the most effective tip and nail placement against the string, and the most effective direction and force of finger movement. Discover the joint positions which give greatest strength and fluency. Constantly strive for maximum ease and security.

When you can securely execute p, i, m, i, practice p, i, a–m, i and p, i–m, a, i–m in a similar manner. You'll find exercises and musical examples for these movement forms in *Part Two*, pp. 77 – 80, 83, and 85 – 86.

A related movement form is p̲, i̲, m̲, i̲, m̲, i̲. This figure has three opposed movements and ends with the same m̲, i̲ sympathetic movement as the preceding p̲, i̲, m̲, i̲ sequence. Also practice the p̲, i̲, a̲–m̲, i̲, a̲–m̲, i̲ and p̲, i̲–m̲, a̲, i̲–m̲, a̲, i̲–m̲ movement forms. As you begin the continuity-stroke, continue to use prepared-strokes for the ascending part of these figures.

You'll find musical examples for these movement forms in *Part Two*, pp. 84 and 87.

# Left-Hand Considerations

As the music you play increases in complexity, so will the movements required by your left-hand fingers. For the most rapid development of coordination and strength, bear in mind the following considerations:

> • **Avoid deviating your wrist, and keep it slightly arched.**
>
> • **Keep your finger joints as close as possible to their mid-range of movement. Avoid collapsing the middle joint as you reach toward the bass side of the fingerboard — especially with the third and fourth fingers.**
>
> • **As you reach across the fingerboard — especially to the bass strings — your fingers will feel as though they're "pulling" your hand. To provide maximum advantage for the fingers, allow your hand, wrist, and forearm to follow this pull freely. (See "Developing Left-Hand Mobility," pp. 93 – 96)**

As you encounter more complex left-hand movement forms, you may want to review the information in "Left-Hand Movement," pp. 45 – 47, and "Movement by Touch: Applying Aim-Directed Movement (ADM)," pp. 47 – 48.

P, i, a introduces a potentially serious problem. Although m is an inactive finger during this movement form, it strongly influences both i and a. If allowed to follow its tendency to remain rigidly extended, m will impede the free movement of i and a. Since there's more independence between m and i than between m and a, you should train m to move with a.

Begin p, i, a in a manner similar to p, i, m (see p. 64). Using prepared-strokes, practice slowly and deliberately. When you're reasonably secure with the prepared-stroke, begin developing the continuity-stroke.

Related movement forms are p, i, a, i and p, i, a, i, a, i. Again, train m to move with a. This creates an opposed movement between i and m, which is much freer than an opposed movement between m and a.

You'll find musical examples for these movement forms in *Part Two*, pp. 90 – 93.

## Alternating I and M on Adjacent Strings

Alternating i and m on adjacent strings should present no problem — it's simply a matter of dropping p from the p, i, m, i, m, i movement form. No changes in your hand position or finger movements are necessary.

## Alternating I and M on a Single String

Because of their different effective reaches, you can alternate i and m more easily when sounding adjacent strings — this is why you began i and m alternation on adjacent strings. But when correctly alternating i and m on the same string, i's middle joint will always be less flexed than m's, even when your hand is correctly tilted. Since i has a shorter reach than m, this is unavoidable.

You should realize, however, that free-stroke requires keeping the middle joint sufficiently flexed for your fingertip to clear the lower adjacent string. A finger can function with *more* flexion than it needs to clear an adjacent string, but it can't function efficiently with *less*. Thus, you should position your hand to allow ideal flexion for the middle joint of i (the finger of shorter reach), and train m (the finger of longer reach) to work in a somewhat more flexed position.

In i and m free-stroke, there are two undesirable consequences of placing the middle joint of i in an insufficiently flexed position:

1) After sounding a string, you unintentionally strike the lower adjacent string with i.
2) To clear the lower adjacent string, you execute an opposed joint movement with i, extending the knuckle while flexing the middle joint. This increases tension, impedes coordination, and yields a weak tone.

To avoid these problems when alternating i and m on a single string, your aims are as follows:

> • **To establish and maintain a sufficiently flexed position of the i middle joint — this ensures that i will clear the lower adjacent string.**
>
> • **To train m to operate in its more flexed position.**

Single-string alternation derives from the now-familiar adjacent-string alternation. Proceed as follows:

❑ **Begin by playing the familiar p, i, m, i arpeggio, sounding ⑤, ③, ②, ③. Then, without pausing, sound ③ several times by alternating i and m.** *Don't alter the position of your hand over the strings.* **Maintain the advantageous position of i — this will cause m to function in a slightly more flexed position.**

❑ **To help compensate for the difference in reaches of i and m, keep your hand properly tilted to the left.**

❏ **When you're reasonably secure with this movement, practice sounding ② with i and m. As before, begin with the p, i, m, i arpeggio, this time sounding ⑤, ②, ①, ②.**

❏ **As you become secure with alternation positioning and movement, gradually work toward the continuity-stroke. Strive for a smooth opposed movement, eliminating any pause at the limits of flexion and extension.**

You'll find musical examples for alternation on a single string in *Part Two*, pp. 99 – 101.

∞　　∞　　∞　　∞　　∞　　∞　　∞

In the foregoing procedure, you began by alternating on ③ and ②, then changed to single-string alternation by reaching with m to ③. Since i remained within its midrange of movement, no change in your hand position was necessary.

*But if you alternate on ③ and ②, and then change to single-string alternation on ②, you must lower your hand position the distance of one string to maintain the midrange movement of i.* If you tried to reach with i to a *higher* adjacent string, i would be forced to function in a more extended position — this would require you to execute an opposed-joint movement with i to avoid brushing against the lower adjacent string.

Only by shifting the position of your hand can you maintain i within its midrange. Thus, you need to understand the technique of string crossing.

# Principles of String Crossing

*String crossing* is the technique of shifting your right hand across the strings to maintain the optimum position of your fingers. In i and m alternation, for example, i should always maintain a sufficiently flexed position at its middle joint to achieve maximum leverage — m will function in a slightly more flexed position. Thus, when i moves to an adjacent string, you must shift your hand across the strings to maintain the optimum position of i. Secure string crossing is essential for executing rapid and accurate scales. In fact, a lack of speed or fluency in playing scales can often be traced to faulty string-crossing technique.

String crossing can be done in various ways — not all of them equally secure and efficient. As a result, students are often confused about how to execute string crossing. Thus, you need to evaluate the possible ways in which string crossing can be executed:

1) moving only from the elbow
2) moving simultaneously from the shoulder and elbow
3) flexing or extending the wrist
4) deviating the wrist to the right or left
5) extending or flexing the middle and knuckle joints beyond their optimum playing positions
6) various combinations of the above

By applying the Principles of Efficient Muscle Function, you can determine which of these possibilities is the most secure and efficient way to execute string crossing.

Deviating your wrist from its advantageous position contradicts the Muscular Alignment Principle — this eliminates the fourth possibility. Flexing or extending your finger joints or wrist contradicts the Midrange Principle — this eliminates the third and fifth possibilities.

Now consider the remaining possibilities:

1) moving only from the elbow
2) moving from the shoulder and elbow.

Like every other aspect of guitar technique, string crossing should be done as simply as possible. Since moving from the elbow alone involves only one joint, it's simpler than moving from the shoulder and elbow. *Thus, as a basic technique, string crossing should be done by moving only from the elbow.*

To alter tone color, advanced guitarists will use subtle shoulder movements in their string-crossing technique. For now, however, you should aim to establish a secure basic technique which you can carry out by habit. String crossing only from your elbow gives you a secure basis from which you can depart when necessary.

# Beginning String Crossing

String crossing often involves moving from one string to an adjacent string. In beginning string crossing, however, the distance between adjacent strings is too small for you to feel the crossing movement clearly. You need to begin with arm movements large enough for you to feel the movement at your elbow clearly. Thus, you'll begin by moving across all six strings.

Using i and m alternation, proceed as follows:

❑ **Prepare i on ① in its optimum position for free-stroke — m will function in a slightly more flexed position.**

❑ **Begin slowly counting aloud in threes ("one, two, three, one, two, three," etc.).**

❑ **Using i, m, i alternation with prepared free-strokes, sound ① three times as you count aloud.**

❑ ***With your wrist and hand held steady*, execute three forearm movements as you continue counting. (Your fingers should not touch the strings during these movements.)**

| | |
|---|---|
| "one": | up precisely the distance of six strings |
| "two": | down the distance of six strings |
| "three": | back up and prepare i on ⑥ |

At the count of three, your hand and wrist should be in position to sound ⑥ with prepared-strokes. *Move only from your elbow — your hand, wrist, and shoulder joint positions should remain unchanged.*

❑ Using i̲, m̲, i̲ alternation, sound ⑥ three times as you count.

❑ With your wrist held steady, execute three forearm movements as you count:

| | |
|---|---|
| "one": | down precisely the distance of six strings |
| "two": | up the distance of six strings |
| "three": | back down and prepare i̲ on ① |

At the count of three, you should be in position to sound ① with prepared free-strokes. *Again, move only from your elbow — your hand and wrist positions should remain unchanged.* **This completes one cycle of the string-crossing exercise.**

Remember, your aim is to establish a secure basic technique which you can carry out by habit. Repeat this exercise — slowly at first, then gradually faster — until you can do it steadily and accurately at a fairly rapid tempo (M.M. ♩ = 92+). When you become secure moving across six strings, gradually decrease the distance of string crossing: moving across five strings, then four, then three, then finally two. As you gradually decrease the distance, you should still clearly feel the movement at your elbow.

You'll find musical examples for string crossing in *Part Two,* pp. 103 – 109.

# *Clarity on Wound Strings*

Bass strings consist of metal windings around a core of nylon fibers. If, when sounding a wound string, you allow your nail to slide even a short distance along the length of the string, it will scrape across the windings. This produces a rasping noise, and can also cause rapid nail wear.

If you have this problem, its solution will become evident when you clearly understand the cause. Carry out the following experiment:

❑ **Prepare i on ⑥ — *this is the contact point.* Note the position of i's middle joint.**

❑ **Begin to execute a stroke very slowly. Notice that, as you flex the middle joint of i, your nail scrapes along the string — this causes the rasping noise.**

❑ **When your finger has moved almost to the point where the string will depart from your nail, pause again — *this is the departure point.* Notice how much more the middle joint of i is flexed than it was at the contact point.**

❑ **Continue the stroke, causing the string to depart from your nail, thus sounding the string. Notice that there was little or no noise — although your nail crossed the string at a slight angle, it didn't slide along the length of the string.**

To eliminate a rasping noise on the wound strings, your fingertip and nail should contact and depart the string *at the same point.* **Thus, you must accurately flex the middle joint to place your tip and nail precisely at the departure point.**

You'll need careful practice to acquire habits of consistent and accurate placement. The results, however, are well worth the effort. Eliminating wasted motion is equally important on every string and benefits your overall right-hand technique. Thus, not only will your tone on the wound strings be clear, but your speed and accuracy with all finger movements will improve substantially.

# Sounding a Single Note Free-Stroke on an Adjacent String

If, when alternating i and m on a single string, you need to sound a higher adjacent string only once, arrange the fingering to sound the higher string with m. Since m is already in an optimum position to sound the higher string, no change in your hand position is necessary. Never use i to sound a higher adjacent string only once — this would require you to quickly shift your hand the distance of one string and back again. Not only would this be awkward, but it would also impair your right-hand security.

If, when alternating i and m on a single string, you need to sound a lower adjacent string only once, sound the lower string with i. Since i can reach the lower string with only a slight increase in flexion, no change in your hand position is necessary. Never use m to sound a lower adjacent string only once — again, this would require you to quickly shift your hand the distance of one string and back again.

You'll sometimes encounter passages in which it's awkward to use m to play a single note on a higher adjacent string. In these situations, use a to sound the higher string:

# <u>M</u> and <u>A</u> Alternation

Since you began <u>i</u> and <u>m</u> alternation on adjacent strings, you might assume that you would begin <u>a</u> and <u>m</u> alternation in the same manner. In normal playing position, however, there are essential differences between these two movement forms. Because of these differences, it's much easier to begin <u>m</u> and <u>a</u> alternation on a single string. To understand why, consider the following:

---

**<u>I</u> and <u>M</u> Alternation:**

Since the knuckle of <u>i</u> is positioned *higher* than the knuckle of <u>m</u>, the reaches of these two fingers are different. Thus, the following are true:

a. In *single-string* alternation, <u>m</u> must function in the flexion side of its midrange to avoid forcing <u>i</u> to function in an extended position.

b. In *adjacent-string* alternation, <u>m</u> can function in its optimum midrange without altering the optimum position of <u>i</u>.

---

*Thus, it's easier to begin <u>i</u> and <u>m</u> alternation on adjacent strings — both <u>i</u> and <u>m</u> can maintain their optimum positions.*

---

**<u>M</u> and <u>A</u> Alternation:**

Although <u>a</u> is shorter than <u>m</u>, the knuckle of <u>a</u> is positioned *lower* than the knuckle of <u>m</u>, so the reaches of these two fingers are approximately equal. Thus the following are true:

a. In *adjacent-string* alternation, <u>m</u> must function in the flexion side of its midrange to avoid forcing <u>a</u> to function in an extended position.

b. In *single-string* alternation, <u>m</u> can function in its optimum midrange without altering the optimum position of <u>a</u>.

---

*Thus, it's easier to begin <u>m</u> and <u>a</u> alternation on a single string — both <u>m</u> and <u>a</u> can maintain their optimum positions.*

You can determine the correct position of the hand and fingers for m and a alternation through the following procedure:

❑ **Using prepared-strokes, sound ② several times with both m and a simultaneously. Find the middle-joint positions in which both fingers can flex sufficiently to clear the lower adjacent string.**

❑ **Sound ② with m and a alternation. (Don't neglect the inactive fingers: i should move with m, and c should move with a.)**

When you can securely execute m and a alternation, practice the string crossing exercises in *Part Two* with m and a.

# Developing Right-Hand Speed

Right-hand speed depends entirely on coordination. The coordination required for right-hand speed can be divided into two categories:

> • Control for accuracy
>
> • Independence for freedom of movement

Independence refers to movement between adjacent fingers, and also to movement between the knuckle and middle joints of a single finger. Since independence is useless without secure habits of control, you've concentrated mainly on control. In each new right-hand movement form, you began by carefully practicing with the prepared-stroke. As you gradually acquired control, you then developed the continuity-stroke. In acquiring control, you've also acquired some degree of independence.

Right-hand speed, however, requires a higher level of independence. Since you haven't yet concentrated on developing independence, you've deferred considerations of speed. Now, assuming your development of control is well under way, you can focus on improving your finger independence.

## Developing Independence through Opposed-Finger Sweep Exercises

At this point, trying to maintain control while developing independence would be too complex. *Opposed-finger sweeps* allow you to concentrate solely on developing independence without the demand for careful control.

Finger sweeps are exercises in which the right-hand fingers are alternately flexed and extended against the resistance of the strings. *Sweeps are not an exercise in relaxation — they're a rigorous exercise.* Perform sweeps vigorously, emphasizing strong and crisp movement at the middle joints. If your hand becomes tired, take a short break. You'll find that several short sessions are more beneficial than one long session.

To help acquire the coordination necessary for opposed-finger sweeps, you'll begin with single-finger sweeps. Proceed as follows:

❑ **With your wrist properly aligned and arched, assume the normal playing position. To provide stability, rest p on ④ or ⑤.**

❑ **To emphasize movement at the middle joints, place your knuckles in a well-extended position.**

❑ **Beginning with i, vigorously flex and extend your finger across the first three or four strings. (Dampen the sound by laying your left-hand fingers across the strings between the 9th and 12th frets.) Follow through fully at the middle joint. There should be only a little movement at the knuckle, but don't hold the knuckle rigid. Keep the inactive fingers slightly flexed.**

❑ **Your finger should firmly brush the strings in both directions. *Emphasize extension!***

❑ **When you're comfortable with i, practice with m, then a.**

When you're reasonably comfortable with the single-finger sweeps, begin practicing the opposed-finger sweeps. These introduce the element of alternation, and thus are extremely beneficial to your development of right-hand speed. *Remember, one finger simultaneously extends as the other flexes.*

❑ **Alternate i and m(a–c). Vigorously sweep the strings in both directions. Again, keep the knuckles well extended (but not rigid). Emphasize movement at the middle joints — your hand should remain steady, without bouncing outward.**

❑ **Next practice alternating m and a.**

❑ **Next practice alternating m and i–a. This is the most challenging and beneficial of opposed-finger sweeps. Again, carefully emphasize extension.**

Practice these exercises slowly and deliberately at first. Always emphasize the following as you practice sweeps:

> • **Keep your knuckles well extended to emphasize movement at the middle joints.**
>
> • **Keep your hand steady — don't allow it to bounce outward.**

As your coordination develops, increase the speed of your sweeps. If your muscles begin to tighten, however, slow down — you need more practice at a slower speed. Acquiring independence is a gradual process, and it may be some time before you can execute sweeps with freedom and ease.

As you gain proficiency, you can practice sweeps either lightly or forcefully, depending on what you wish to emphasize:

> • **Practice lightly to develop speed.**
>
> • **Practice forcefully to build strength and endurance.**

# Integrating Independence and Control

In addition to developing independence through sweeps, you also need to develop control. Thus, you need to begin practicing various right-hand movement forms in a way which gradually improves your ability to control movement accurately at a fast tempo.

To play rapidly, you have to practice playing rapidly. You can do this by carefully experimenting with the limits of your control. The following procedure can be carried out with any right-hand movement form:

❑ Using the metronome, gradually increase your speed to just past the point where you begin to lose control — this will define the limit of your right-hand speed. Then slow down slightly to the fastest tempo at which you can play accurately.

❑ Practice at this tempo for as long as you feel necessary — *you should be able to maintain acceptable control.*

❑ When you feel reasonably secure and confident at this tempo, gradually increase your speed again to just past the point where you begin to lose control:

a. If you lose control at the same tempo as you did before, you need more repetitions at your original practice tempo.

b. If you lose control at a slightly faster tempo than before, this defines the new limit of your right-hand speed. Slow down slightly and find the new tempo at which you can play with both speed and control.

❑ Repeat the previous steps. *Your aim is to gradually push the limits of your ability to play with speed and control.* With time and sufficient practice, you'll gradually increase your right-hand speed.

# *Summary*

Students who develop correct habits of movement usually have little trouble developing the coordination to play rapidly. Emphasize the following as you practice right-hand speed:

> • **Extension and flexion of the fingers as directly as possible**
>
> • **Freedom of movement at the middle joints**
>
> • **Correct positioning and movement of the inactive fingers relative to the active fingers**

Remember, the essentials of right-hand speed are control and independence of joint movement. To play rapidly, you need a balance between these two essentials. Alternately practice control and independence until they become integrated. You could accurately call this "controlled independence."

# Comparing Rest-Stroke and Free-Stroke

Before you begin advanced study of the rest-stroke and free-stroke, it will help to understand the differences between them. The better you understand these differences, the easier and more rapid your development will be.

Generally, the free-stroke has broader musical application and provides an easier approach to alternation than the rest-stroke. But during forte playing, a well-developed rest-stroke gives more volume and fullness of tone than even the best-developed free-stroke. This makes the rest-stroke an effective expressive device.

The rest-stroke's advantages derive largely from two characteristics not shared by the free-stroke:

**1) In rest-stroke, you sound the string near the end of its movement — *after* your finger has gained momentum and power. In free-stroke, you sound the string near the beginning of its movement — *before* your finger has gained momentum or power. Thus, in the rest-stroke, the advantages of momentum and power are available at the best possible time — at the instant you sound the string.**

**2) In rest-stroke, your finger comes to rest on the adjacent string, giving the movement a secure point of culmination. Thus, the rest-stroke provides an extra element of security, gives an added feeling of freedom, and yields fewer problems of accuracy and tone.**

These advantages do not imply that you can't get a good tone with free-stroke. During normal playing, you should be able to produce a similar tone with free-stroke and rest-stroke. Also, the free-stroke has practical advantages which shouldn't be ignored — it's the more legato and versatile of strokes, equally useful for scales, arpeggios, and chords.

# *Rest-Stroke Finger Alternation*

As you begin rest-stroke alternation, remember that your fingers must move in opposite directions — one finger simultaneously extending as the other flexes.

While your ultimate goal in alternation is speed, this should not be your immediate concern. For now, you should concentrate on developing the coordination essential for rest-stroke alternation. Also, since the prepared-stroke would prevent you from developing the necessary momentum for the rest-stroke, use the continuity-stroke. Practice as slowly as necessary for firm and accurate placement against the strings, but maintain the continuous motion of the continuity-stroke.

You'll begin rest-stroke alternation with i and m on ②. Proceed as follows:

❏ **In positioning the middle joints of i and m, you must strike a compromise to gain maximum advantage for both fingers: i (the finger of shorter reach) will be *extended* slightly past its midway position, and m will be *flexed* slightly past its midway position.**

❏ **Place m securely against ③. Extend the knuckle and middle joints of i so that its tip is approximately 3/8" from ②.**

❏ **Flex i; as i contacts ②, extend m without a pause. As i sounds ② and follows through to come to rest against ③, m should continue extending to a position approximately 3/8" from ②.**

❏ **Without hesitation, complete the alternation cycle by sounding ② with m and simultaneously extending i. *Keep a and c slightly more flexed and moving with m.***

❏ **If your nail tends to catch on the string, try one or any combination of the following:**

    a. **As your finger contacts the string, use more tip and less nail.**
    b. **Begin the stroke with the middle joint slightly more extended.**
    c. **Allow the tip joint to give slightly.**
    d. **Use shorter nails.**

**(Generally, these need only be temporary solutions — the problem of catching your nail on a string usually disappears as you acquire sufficient coordination.)**

❑ **When you're reasonably secure with i̲ and m̲ alternation, practice m̲ and a̲ in a similar manner.**

As you acquire coordination with rest-stroke alternation, you should gradually accelerate the movements. For more volume, you can slightly increase the extension of each finger to gain more momentum when sounding the strings.

Carefully listen to your tone. You may need to experiment further with nail lengths and shapes (see "Nail Contours and Suggested Shapings," pp. 24 – 27). Although short nails require more accurate finger movements, they allow you to sound the strings with firmer tip joints. Thus, for a crisper and more powerful tone in both rest-stroke and free-stroke, try keeping your nails relatively short.

You'll find musical exercises for developing rest-stroke alternation in *Part Two,* beginning on p. 112.

# Sounding Three Strings Together with P̲ and the Fingers

Whether sounding three strings together or in succession, the basic free-stroke for p̲ and the fingers is the same. When p̲ and the fingers flex simultaneously, however, your hand may tend to spring outward from the wrist. There are two main causes of this tendency:

• **Too much flexion at the knuckles**

• **Insufficient flexion and follow-through at the middle joints**

Uncorrected, this tendency will hinder your development of right-hand accuracy and tone production. You can correct it through careful and deliberate practice. Proceed as follows, beginning with p̲–i̲–m̲ sounding ⑤–③–②:

❑ **Prepare p–i–m on their respective strings.**

❑ **Sound the strings simultaneously — emphasize follow-through at the middle joints and sharply limit movement at the knuckles. Also emphasize the follow-through of p. As always, keep a-c slightly flexed and moving with m.**

❑ **When you're reasonably secure with the prepared-stroke, begin using the continuity-stroke.**

As you gain coordination, you'll gradually need less effort to keep your right hand steady. You'll find musical examples for developing the p–i–m movement form in *Part Two*, pp. 120 – 122.

## Sounding Two Strings Together with P and One Finger

When moving p and one finger together, students often find an even stronger tendency of the hand to spring outward than during p–i–m. During p–i–m, the inactive fingers tend to move with the active fingers, so p–i–m presents fewer problems of coordination and stability. When moving p and one finger, however, the inactive fingers tend to remain extended — impeding the movement of the active finger. Thus, you must give special attention to the inactive fingers when moving p and one finger together.

Begin with p and m sounding ⑤ and ② (free-stroke). Apply the same procedure as you did for p–i–m, and carefully observe the following:

- **For security and the best tone, begin with the prepared-stroke.**

- **Emphasize middle joint movement and follow-through of the fingers.**

- **P should follow through freely, coming to rest against i.**

- **Keep the inactive fingers moving with m.**

When you're reasonably secure with p–m, practice p–i and p–a. You'll find musical examples for these movement forms in *Part Two*, pp. 123 – 124.

# P, I, M, A

Practice p, i, m, a in a manner similar to p, i, m–a (see pp. 65 – 66). Remember to position a for maximum advantage.

You'll find musical examples for this movement form in *Part Two*, pp. 136 – 145.

# P, I, M, A, M, I

❑ **Prepare p on ⑤ and i–m–a on ③, ②, ①.**

❑ **Sound ⑤ with p, followed by ③ with i.**

❑ **As i follows through, flex m sympathetically with i to sound ②.**

❑ **Flex a to sound ① while simultaneously preparing i–m on ③ and ②.**

❑ **As a follows through, flex m sympathetically with a to sound ②.**

❑ **Flex i sympathetically with m to sound ③ while simultaneously preparing p on ⑤.**

❑ **Flex p to sound ⑤ while simultaneously preparing i–m–a on ③, ②, ①.**

❑ **As always, c should move with a.**

Considering the complexity of this arpeggio figure, a quick review of the prepared-stroke will be helpful:

> • The prepared-stroke is invaluable for helping you develop secure habits of firm tip and nail placement against the string. These habits are the foundation of good tone production.
>
> • The prepared-stroke helps you develop the finger independence essential for playing the guitar well.
>
> • It speeds your progress toward developing a secure continuity-stroke.
>
> • The security gained through the prepared-stroke contributes strongly to your confidence as a performer.

You'll find musical examples for p, i, m, a, m, i in *Part Two*, p. 138.

## Four Strings Simultaneously with P–I–M–A

The previous consideration of emphasizing the sound produced by a still applies (see p. 62). Thus, you should flex p–i–m relatively gently and carefully emphasize a's firm placement, flexion, and follow-through.

Begin by isolating and practicing this technique — perhaps on open strings. When you feel reasonably secure, you can further develop this technique by playing simple music consisting largely of chords in which the highest note must be emphasized. Developing the independence and control of a takes time, but it's essential if you're to become a proficient guitarist. Here again, the prepared-stroke will prove invaluable.

You'll find musical examples for developing this technique in *Part Two*, pp. 152 – 159.

# Further Left-Hand Training

The Principles of Efficient Muscle Function apply in different ways to the right and left hands. The right-hand thumb and finger movements needed to play the guitar allow you not only to keep your right hand in a relatively stable position, but also to use the most advantageous movements when sounding the strings. Your left hand, however, must frequently execute movements and positions which don't entirely conform to the principles. But you can still use the principles as a point of departure, aiming for the least strenuous, most controlled, and most comfortable movements and positions. (Before proceeding, be certain you understand "The Four Principles of Efficient Muscle Function," pp. 9 – 11.)

## Applying the Principles of Efficient Muscle Function

Each of the four principles has specific applications to your left hand.

**Muscular Alignment:** Never deviate your left-hand wrist. When moving from one position to another on the fingerboard, move your arm laterally from your shoulder joint. Although lateral spreading of your fingers is sometimes necessary, you can often minimize it by rotating your forearm clockwise to increase the angle at which your fingers approach the strings (see Figure 35B, p. 95).

**Midrange Function of Joints:** This is indispensable for minimizing tension. Although the Midrange Function Principle can always be applied to the wrist, it can't always be applied to the fingers. It can be applied often enough, however, for you to establish a powerful *basic* left-hand position. You can use this basic position as a point of departure whenever the music requires a movement form which contradicts this principle.

**Uniform Direction of Joint Movement:** When well coordinated, finger joints tend to move in a uniform direction. Although you can't always apply this principle, you should keep it in mind and apply it whenever possible.

***Follow-Through:*** As a finger flexes to depress a string, it must continually apply force against the fingerboard. Thus, since there's no follow-through to consider, the Follow-Through Principle isn't a consideration when flexing a finger to depress a string.[†]

When applied to left-hand *extension,* the Follow-Through Principle is subtle. Some guitarists believe that the fingers, when extending from the frets and into their inactive positions, should be held as closely as possible to the fingerboard. But this is a misapplication of the "economy-of-movement" idea.[††] A feeling of minimal tension is the best criterion for how far to lift your fingers. Don't overextend your fingers, but don't restrain them either. To gain left-hand speed and mobility, your fingers must move sufficiently to promote muscular release.

∾ ∾ ∾ ∾ ∾ ∾ ∾

Another consideration, though not directly related to the Principles of Efficient Muscle Function, is the amount of pressure you use when depressing the strings. At all times, avoid pressing the strings harder than necessary — use only enough pressure to get a clear sound. By generally observing these principles, you can reduce left-hand tension and fatigue.

## Developing Left-Hand Mobility

*Left-hand mobility* refers to the free positioning of your hand to provide maximum advantage for the involved muscles as you execute left-hand movement forms. Left-hand mobility includes all movements of your arm, wrist, and fingers.[†††]

---

[†]*To the teacher:* In downward technical slurs, of course, there is follow-through during flexion. But this follow-through generally occurs so naturally that it seldom requires any attention.
[††]See "Economy of Movement," p. 122.
[†††]*To the teacher:* Left-hand mobility also includes shifting. Shifting, however, is an advanced technique — thus, it will not be addressed in *Part One.*

In considering left-hand mobility, a review of the considerations provided on p. 70 will be helpful:

> • **As a basic technique, avoid deviation or hyperextension of your wrist.**
>
> • **For maximum leverage, do not allow the middle or tip joints of the fingers to collapse — be sure to pay particular attention to the third and fourth fingers.**
>
> • **Let the pull of your fingers determine the position of your hand. Freely rotate your forearm and allow your elbow to move out or in to achieve maximum ease for your fingers.**

These considerations allow your fingers to function with maximum, well-balanced mechanical advantage and no excess tension.

You can move your left hand in the following ways:

1) by rotating your forearm
2) by moving your arm sideways, forward, or backward from your shoulder
3) by flexing, extending, or deviating your wrist
4) by flexing or extending your elbow
5) by combining any of the above

Although some movement forms require little or no mobility, others require considerable mobility. With proper training, you'll respond automatically to these movement forms, allowing your hand, wrist, and arm to follow the pull of your fingers. The following musical examples demand considerable left-hand mobility:

A.                    B.                    C.

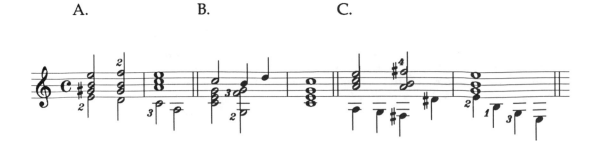

You should play the first and third chords of each example with your wrist and arm in their midrange positions:

*Figure 35A*

The second chord of each example, however, requires you to arch your wrist and rotate your forearm clockwise, causing the knuckle area of your first finger to press gently against the edge of the fingerboard:

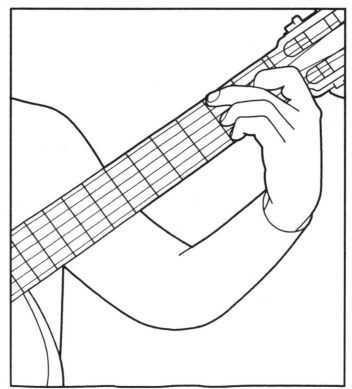

*Figure 35B*

Notice also that, in the second chord of Example A, your first finger acts as a pivot while your second finger moves to F (Fa).

While you should freely apply the concepts of left-hand mobility as you execute movement forms, remember that a single movement form may include more than one finger movement. If you're playing two or more consecutive notes rapidly enough so that they feel like one unified movement — as in a scale fragment — you should consider them to be a single movement form. Thus, your hand position shouldn't favor any single finger — rather, it should provide a balance of muscular advantage for all fingers involved in the movement form.

Until you've gained coordination with left-hand mobility, you should evaluate any fingering or hand position by two simple criteria:

> • **Does it work?**
>
> • **Can I move with maximum ease and security?**

As with all other aspects of guitar technique, your goal is to practice left-hand mobility until it becomes habitual.

# Slurs

A *slur* is a curved line between, above, or below two or more successive notes. In guitar music, there are two kinds of slurs:

*Phrasing slur:* This indicates that the notes are to be played as a group.

*Technical slur:* This occurs only between notes of different pitch — it indicates that, after sounding the first note with your right hand, you sound the remaining note with your left hand alone. Older editions indicate the technical slur with a solid curved line:

Newer editions generally indicate the technical slur with a broken curved line:

This clearly distinguishes the technical slur from the phrasing slur and tie.[†]

# *Technical Slurs*

Slurs are either upward or downward, depending on their pitchwise direction of movement. To execute an upward slur, sound a note with the right hand, then rapidly and firmly hammer the vibrating string against the fret with a left-hand finger. The resulting sound comes not only from the string's vibration carried over from the preceding note, but also from the impact of the string against the fret.

To execute a downward slur, sound a note which is formed with a left-hand finger, then pluck the string with the left-hand finger to sound the lower note of the slur.

---

[†]For an explanation of the tie, see *Part Two,* p. 43.

# *Types of Downward Slurs*

There are three types of downward slurs. Each of these slurs is defined by how the finger moves in relation to the higher adjacent string. (Since there's no higher string adjacent to ①, downward slurs on ① are not classified in this way.)

*Rest slur:* The left-hand finger executes the slur parallel to the surface of the fingerboard, coming to rest against the higher adjacent string. Although this is the most powerful slur, it's a very restrictive movement. Thus, the rest slur is most frequently used in slower passages.

*Brush slur:* The left-hand finger lightly brushes the higher adjacent string and passes over it in a follow-through movement. This is the most rapid and practical slur. Since the finger executing the slur brushes against the higher adjacent string, this string must be dampened in one of the following ways:

> • If the slurred note is formed with a finger, lean the finger against the higher adjacent string.
>
> • If the slurred note is an open string, use an inactive left-hand finger to dampen the adjacent higher string.

*Free slur:* The left-hand finger executing the slur plucks sharply outward, passing over the higher adjacent string. The free slur is used when the higher adjacent string must continue sounding. Also, it's the most practical slur when you're barring across six strings.

Although the brush slur is used most often, you may occasionally find the rest and free slurs useful, depending on the speed, dynamics, and left-hand requirements of the music.

You can rapidly develop your slur technique by being sensitive to feelings of strength and ease of execution. Always observe the following as you practice slurs:

> • **For maximum strength and leverage, keep the finger executing the slur curved in its midrange position — this is especially important when slurring with your fourth finger.**
>
> • **In playing the upward slur, don't unnecessarily restrict movement. Lift your fingers enough so that you'll have sufficient downward momentum for "hammering."**
>
> • **Stress sympathetic movements when slurring groups of notes.**

You'll find musical examples for slurring in *Part Two*, pp. 163 – 167.[†]

---

[†]For more detailed slurring exercises, see my *Classic Guitar Technique: Slur, Ornament and Reach Development Exercises*, CPP-Belwin, 15800 N.W. 48th Avenue, Miami, FL 33014.

# Further Right-Hand Training

## *Arpeggios without P*

In arpeggios without p̲, there are five possible fingering combinations:

- **A̲, M̲, I̲**

- **I̲, M̲, A̲**

- **A̲, M̲, I̲, M̲**

- **I̲, A̲, M̲, A̲**

- **A̲, I̲, M̲, I̲**

Each of these can be started on a different finger for different arpeggio figures, but the relationship of finger movements remains the same.

In arpeggios with p̲ and the fingers, flexion of p̲ provides a brief release for the fingers — this helps avoid a build-up of right-hand tension during continuous arpeggios. In arpeggios without p̲, however, this release for the fingers is absent. Thus, to avoid excess tension, you need to consider how the fingers move in relation to each other:

> • As a general rule, since the opposed movement presents more problems of coordination, you should execute it between the more independent i̲ and m̲ whenever possible. You should execute the sympathetic movement between the less independent m̲ and a̲.
>
> • If you must use an opposed movement between a̲ and m̲, immediately follow it with a sympathetic movement. For example, in the p̲, i̲, m̲, a̲, m̲, i̲ arpeggio (see p. 90), a̲ and m̲ require an opposed movement between them. Immediately after alternating with a̲, however, m̲ sounds its string and follows through sympathetically with a̲ — this provides a brief release for a̲ and m̲.

## A, M, I

You'll begin with a, m̲, i sounding ①, ②, ③. *I prepares as m̲ flexes, and a̲–m̲ prepare as i̲ flexes.* As always, c̲ should move with a̲. Proceed as follows:

❑ **Establish the optimum position for a̲ to sound ① (see** p. 61).

❑ **Prepare a̲–m̲ on ① and ②. I̲ should be in a slightly flexed position.**

❑ **Flex a̲ to sound ①.**

❑ **Flex m̲ sympathetically with a̲ to sound ②; as m̲ flexes, simultaneously prepare i̲ on ③.**

❑ **Flex i̲ to sound ③; as i̲ flexes, simultaneously prepare a̲–m̲ on ① and ②.**

❑ **As you carry out this procedure, be sure to firmly flex the middle joint of a̲ to accent ①.**

Through careful repetition, you'll soon begin to automatically execute the sympathetic movement between a̲ and m̲ and the opposed movement between m̲ and i̲. When you're reasonably secure with a̲, m̲, i̲ using prepared-strokes, begin using continuity-strokes.

∾     ∾     ∾     ∾     ∾     ∾     ∾

Depending on which finger you begin with, the a̲, m̲, i̲ arpeggio will also result in m̲, i̲, a̲ and i̲, a̲, m̲. Although these aren't found in guitar music as often as a̲, m̲, i̲, you should eventually practice them. When practicing m̲, i̲, a̲ and i̲, a̲, m̲, you should accent the finger which begins the arpeggio. As before, execute the sympathetic movement between a̲ and m̲, and the opposed movement between a̲–m̲ and i̲.

**CAUTION:** When beginning with m̲ or i̲ (depending on which arpeggio you're practicing), you may tend to neglect the sympathetic movement between m̲ and a̲. Although you're no longer accenting the same finger as in a̲, m̲, i̲, you must continue to properly time the sympathetic movement.

You'll find musical examples for the a̲, m̲, i̲ arpeggio in *Part Two,* pp. 160 – 162 and pp. 188 – 189.

# I̲, M̲, A̲

As in the a̲, m̲, i̲ arpeggio, the i̲, m̲, a̲ arpeggio contains an opposed movement between i̲ and m̲ and a sympathetic movement between m̲ and a̲. *Again, i̲ prepares as m̲ flexes, and a̲–m̲ prepare as i̲ flexes.*

An effective way to approach the i̲, m̲, a̲ arpeggio is to begin with the p̲, m̲, a̲ arpeggio and then, without stopping, substitute i̲ for p̲. Proceed as follows:

❑ **Establish the optimum position for a̲ to sound ①.**

❑ **Prepare p̲ on ④; i̲–m̲–a̲ should be slightly flexed.**

❑ **Flex p̲ to sound ④; as p̲ flexes, simultaneously prepare m̲–a̲ on ② and ①.**

❑ **Flex m̲ to sound ②.**

❑ **Flex a̲ sympathetically with m̲ to sound ①; as a̲ flexes, simultaneously prepare p̲ on ④.**

❑ **Repeat this cycle several times to establish the sympathetic movement between m̲ and a̲.**

❑ **Now, without stopping, substitute i̲ on ③ for p̲ on ④.**

❑ **As you gain security with the prepared-stroke, gradually work toward the continuity-stroke.**

Beginning i, m, a with a different finger results in two more arpeggios: a, i, m and m, a, i. Since, in guitar music, a, i, m is more frequently used than either m, a, i or i, m, a, you should concentrate on developing a, i, m — be sure to accent the tone produced by a.

You'll find musical examples for a, i, m in *Part Two*, pp. 169 – 170 .

# A, M, I, M

The a, m, i, m movement form consists of two sympathetic and two opposed movements. *Always prepare two fingers at a time: i–m when a flexes, and m–a when i flexes.* As always, c should move with a.

Proceed as follows:

❑ **Position a for maximum advantage.**

❑ **Prepare a on ①; i–m should be slightly flexed.**

❑ **Flex a to sound①; as a flexes, simultaneously prepare i–m on③and②.**

❑ **Flex m sympathetically with a to sound②.**

❑ **Flex i to sound ③; as i flexes, simultaneously prepare m–a on②and①.**

❑ **Flex m sympathetically with i to sound②.**

You'll find musical examples for a, m, i, m in *Part Two*, pp. 180 – 181.

# I, A, M, A

The i, a, m, a movement form consists of the following movements:

1) An opposed movement between i and a–m.
2) An opposed movement between a and m.
3) A sympathetic movement between m and a.

Proceed as follows:

❑ **Prepare i on ③ ; m–a should be slightly flexed.**

❑ **Flex i to sound ③ ; as i flexes, prepare m–a on ② and ①.**

❑ **Flex a to sound ①.**

❑ **Flex m to sound ② ; as m flexes, prepare a on ①.**

❑ **Flex a sympathetically with m to sound ① ; as a flexes, prepare i on ③.**

You'll find musical examples for i, a, m, a in *Part Two*, pp. 192 – 193.

# A, I, M, I

The a, i, m, i movement form contains opposed movements between i and m. Using a sympathetic movement between m and i would require an opposed movement of a and m. Thus, a, i, m, i contains no sympathetic movement.

*NOTE: In this movement form, always move a and m together, but prepare only the finger which is about to sound a string.* Proceed as follows:

❑ **Prepare a on ①; i and m should be slightly flexed.**

❑ **Flex a to sound ①; m follows through with a as i extends to prepare on ③.**

❑ **Flex i to sound ③; as i flexes, prepare m on ②.**

❑ **Flex m to sound ②; as m flexes, prepare i on ③.**

❑ **Flex i to sound ③; as i flexes, prepare a on ①.**

You'll find musical examples for a, i, m, i in *Part Two*, p. 200.

# Conditioning and Coordination Exercises

Conditioning and coordination exercises for the hands aren't a new idea — in his 1716 publication of *L'art de Toucher le Clavecin*, French harpsichordist Francois Couperin recommended stretching exercises for the hand muscles. Since then, many performers and teachers have advocated hand exercises for instrumentalists.

Two types of stretching exercises are given here. The first is for improving muscular flexibility and conditioning. The second is for developing control and independence of specific finger joints.

## The Importance of Stretching Exercises

During guitar playing, the stress placed on the small muscles controlling your hands is comparable to the stress placed on larger muscles in the most rigorous sports activities. During a demanding performance or practice session your muscles must repeat movements thousands of times. Many of these movements must be rapid and powerful, and all must be extraordinarily precise. This can leave your muscles feeling sore and stiff — particularly during the early stages of training.

Over the years, sports medicine has given us considerable insight into the conditioning and training of muscles. To be at their best, muscles undergoing intensive training and use require regular stretching exercises. For guitarists, stretching exercises yield a number of benefits:

> • They develop muscular flexibility, allowing your hands to respond more easily to training.
>
> • They minimize muscular soreness and stiffness during training, allowing you to develop coordination more quickly.

• They maintain muscular flexibility after you've gained the coordination to play well.

• They reduce the chances of injury to your muscles and tendons.

# Procedure for Stretching Exercises

The stretching exercises themselves are presented on pp. 108 – 110. The following general procedure should be used with all stretching exercises:

❑ Relax your upper arm, bend your elbow, and allow your wrist to remain collapsed.

❑ While keeping your muscles as relaxed as possible, begin the exercise by pulling slowly. Increase the pull to a point just short of where you feel slight discomfort. CAUTION: Never stretch by jerking the muscles. *If you feel pain, release immediately!*

❑ Pull slowly and steadily for five seconds.

❑ Release and relax for a moment. Repeat the exercise one more time before going on to another finger.

As you feel less discomfort during stretching exercises, gradually increase the duration of each stretch to 30 seconds. Also increase the repetitions and tension of each stretch.

You should do stretching exercises from the beginning of your training. Once your hands develop strength and flexibility, you'll need only one or two brief stretching sessions per day to maintain their conditioning.

Stretching exercises are classified according to the muscles being stretched — either flexors or extensors. Muscles are stretched by pulling them in the direction opposite their function. Thus, flexors are pulled in the direction of extension (away from your body) and extensors are pulled in the direction of flexion (toward your body).

Although only the right hand is illustrated, the exercises which follow should be done with both hands.

**• Flexor stretch of p: Grasp only the tip segment of p and gently pull downward.**

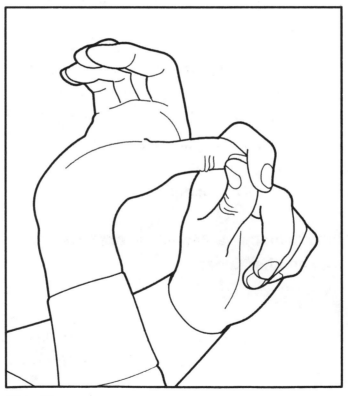

*Figure 36*

• **Flexor stretch of all four fingers while moving p**: Stretch your fingers while fully flexing and extending p. As you count to five, complete one cycle of flexion and extension for each count.

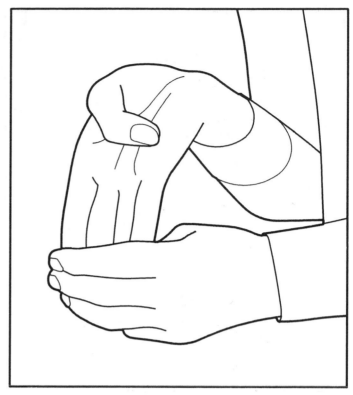

*Figure 37*

• **Flexor stretch** — for your left hand, stretch each finger individually; for your right hand, stretch i and m individually and a–c together:

❑ Beginning with your index finger, stretch each finger individually.

❑ Repeat the exercise — this time, as you stretch a finger, flex and extend the free fingers.

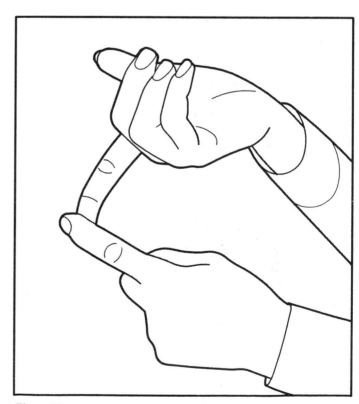

*Figure 38*

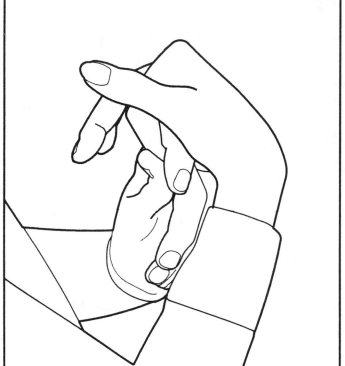

*Figure 39*

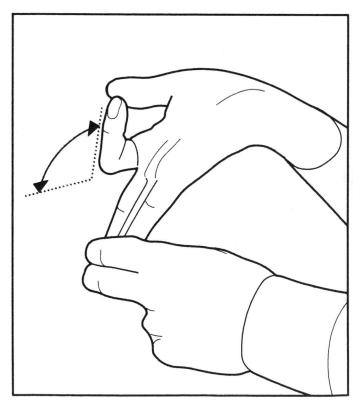

*Figure 40*

• **Extensor stretch — for your left hand, stretch each finger individually; for your right hand, stretch i and m individually and a–c together:**

❑ **Beginning with your index finger, stretch each finger individually.**

❑ **Repeat the exercise — this time, as you stretch a finger, extend and flex the free fingers, emphasizing movement at the knuckles.**

• **Flexor stretch combined with movement of a free finger. Begin with your right hand:**

❑ **Stretch m–a–c while flexing and extending the middle joint of i.**

❑ **Stretch i–a–c while flexing and extending the middle joint of m.**

❑ **Stretch i–m while flexing and extending the middle joints of a–c.**

• **Repeat this exercise with your left hand, training 3 and 4 individually.**

# Developing Muscular Coordination

Although you'll develop muscular coordination largely by practicing with the guitar, you can accelerate this development with exercises away from the guitar. By setting aside the guitar, you can concentrate specifically on developing independence and control of your middle and knuckle joints. The more basic coordination you gain away from the guitar, the easier, faster, and more rewarding your progress will be on the guitar.

Independence and control are the two essentials of coordination (see p. 81). You can develop them most efficiently by observing the following considerations with all coordination exercises:

> • Relax your upper arm, and flex your forearm to a horizontal position. Rotate your forearm, and carefully maintain the alignment and arch of your wrist, as though your hand were in playing position. Keep your thumb as relaxed as possible.
>
> • Execute each exercise movement five times — then fully relax your hand and arm for a moment.

You should begin by emphasizing gentle movement and control rather than speed. At first, these coordination exercises may cause some muscular soreness and stiffness — thus, you may wish to begin and end each session with stretching exercises. As you gain freedom and ease with each coordination exercise, add more repetitions, and increase the speed until you reach a level of moderate fatigue.

## Coordination Exercises

• **Movement of a single finger (see Figure 41):**

❑ Extend all four fingers.

❑ While keeping m–a–c and the knuckle joint of i stationary, flex and extend the middle joint of i. Carefully avoid pulling i sideways.

❑ Carry this out with m while keeping i–a–c stationary, then with a–c while keeping i–m stationary.

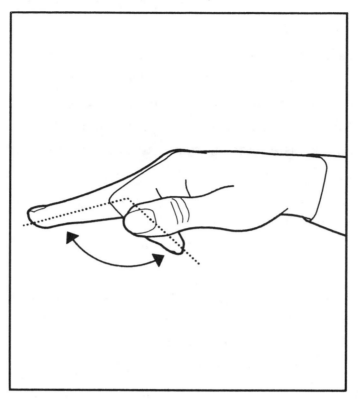

*Figure 41*

• **Alternation:**

❑ Follow the procedure for the preceding exercise. Now, however, alternate i and m–a–c, flexing and extending from the middle joints.

❑ Next, alternate i–m and a–c.

❑ Now, keep a–c extended and stationary while alternating i and m at their middle joints — keep the knuckles of i and m stationary.

❑ Next, alternate m and a–c while keeping i extended.

❑ Next, alternate i and a–c while keeping m extended.

❑ Now for the most challenging (and beneficial) exercise — alternate m with i–a–c. Keep your knuckle joints firmly extended, and emphasize precise movement at the middle joints.

# The Remedial Student

You're a remedial student if the following statements apply to you:

> - **You've tried to learn the guitar.**
>
> - **You're unable to play with security and confidence.**
>
> - **You're seeking a more effective approach to learning the guitar.**

Many students begin remedial study for a specific reason. Perhaps they have technical deficiencies which cause them to make errors. Perhaps they have trouble memorizing music. Or maybe they suffer from performance anxiety. Whatever their reasons, they often begin remedial study expecting to improve a single aspect of their development.

Insecurity, however, is never isolated to a single aspect of development. If you're insecure in one area of guitar study, insecurity will automatically hamper your overall ability to perform. You must constantly strive for security and confidence in every area of guitar study. Thus, the changes you need to make may be more extensive than you first anticipated.

For guitarists, remedial study is the norm rather than the exception. Few guitarists have had good early training. Even in colleges and conservatories, most students spend considerable time in remedial study. Further, you shouldn't assume that remedial study means you have only limited potential. Many of today's finest guitarists were once remedial students.

As you begin remedial study, be aware of the following considerations:

### • *Concentrate only on what you need to do here and now.*

Students are under constant pressure to measure up. Sometimes this pressure is imposed on them by others — this is especially true in colleges and conservatories, where students are faced with grades, recitals, juries, and competitions. Often, however, students pressure themselves. They hear other students playing virtuoso pieces. They've read about virtuosi who gave their first recitals at an early age. Students tend to expect that, if they've been playing for years, they should be able to play challenging music.

This pressure to measure up can be highly destructive to the development of security and confidence. It often compels students to attempt music that's beyond their capabilities, thus breeding impatience, frustration, and failure.

Evaluate your capabilities honestly and dispassionately. This may be disturbing at first — you may find that you cannot accurately play even simple pieces with ease. But don't be discouraged. This is a necessary step in your development. The first step toward improvement is understanding what you can and cannot do, regardless of what other students are doing. Begin from where you are — not from where you think you ought to be.

### • *Make a clean break with your old way of playing and performing.*

Students undergoing extensive remedial study sometimes assume that they can continue to play their familiar repertoire, jobs, or even formal concerts. This is a serious mistake. You can't establish beneficial habits if you're continually reinforcing old habits.

If you must make extensive changes, don't continue playing your familiar repertoire — work only with new music. Further, if you're playing concerts or a job, stop immediately. Always remember, you're striving to establish new habits of security and confidence, and your mind and muscles respond only to what you actually do. Thus, you shouldn't try to perform until you've securely established these new habits.

∾     ∾     ∾     ∾     ∾     ∾     ∾

In my experience, the hardest thing for remedial students to do is to recognize the limitations of their old habits. Although they understand the need for remedial study, they don't see why they should give up their old repertoire, and they resist changing the way they've always practiced.

If you're unsure of how extensively you need to pursue remedial study, ask yourself the following questions:

> • Can I perform my old repertoire in a way which is acceptable to me?
>
> • Did my old way of practicing result in acceptable progress?

You should pursue remedial study to the extent that you're dissatisfied with your old way of practicing and performing — if your old way is unacceptable to you, then you should make the cleanest possible break from it.

A further caution: As you begin remedial study, all your experience may tell you that something's amiss. Remedial study feels wrong — it's too difficult — it may work for others, but it won't work for you. This reaction is entirely natural. Bear in mind that your attitudes and expectations have been shaped by your previous study. Thus, anything new — regardless of its potential benefits — will feel wrong at first.

*You must strive to avoid all negative attitudes and expectations. Allow sufficient time for new movements and thought processes to become habitual — only then will you be able to experience the benefits of remedial study.*

## Summary

Remedial study requires mental stamina and tenacity. You must study and practice in a way which is new to you. You'll need to redefine your attitude toward the guitar, your listeners, and yourself. Perhaps nothing you've ever done has required such a profound personal change.

*But it can be done!* Many remedial students have learned to perform with security and confidence. Some have gone on to become brilliant concert artists. Thus, you have every reason for optimism.

Each procedure in *Learning the Classic Guitar* is designed to increase your security and confidence as a performer. But these procedures are of little value without your time and effort. Your ultimate development will be directly related to the care and attention you devote to remedial study.

Become a scholar of the guitar. Strive to understand the reasons behind each procedure. The more sensitive you become to the potential benefits of each procedure, the more fully you'll be able to realize them.

# The Natural Approach

"Natural" is a word which often appears in guitar instruction. Generally, everyone agrees that the guitar should be learned in the most natural way possible. Students progress more easily and quickly if they take advantage of how the body naturally functions — both mentally and physically. Thus, "natural" can be defined as follows:

> **"Natural" and "efficient" are synonymous — the most natural approach is the one which produces the most secure and rapid progress for the time applied in study and practice.**

There's little agreement, however, on what constitutes a natural approach to learning to play the guitar. Different guitarists have developed different — in some cases, contradictory — approaches. Yet most would assert that their approach, if not the most natural, is at least as natural as any other.

Is this assertion true? Can different approaches be equally natural? In practical application, the answer is "no." The reason becomes clear if you consider the following:

> **• Although individuals vary from person to person, we are far more alike than different. Physically, we function most efficiently by observing basic principles of positioning and movement. Psychologically, we learn most efficiently by avoiding confusion and error — by acquiring habits of understanding, accuracy, security, and confidence.**
>
> **• Every guitar student shares the same basic aim: to acquire the physical and mental abilities needed for securely performing music.**
>
> **In light of these indisputable similarities, different approaches cannot be equally natural.**

**Thus, we need criteria which will enable us to recognize the most natural approach.**

## *Determining the Most Natural Approach*

We can determine whether we're approaching the guitar in the most natural way through the following criteria:

---

### 1) How We Naturally Learn:

• We must constantly be aware of the importance and inevitability of habits. Every thought and action contributes to a habit. Thus, we must always practice with the clear intention of acquiring effective habits of thought and movement.

• We must be equally aware of the importance of concentration. A wandering mind hinders the process of learning. Thus, we must develop the ability to maintain clear and sustained concentration.

• We must avoid confusion and error.

### 2) How We Naturally Move:

• The mind controls the muscles. Thus, we must proceed with clear aims of movement.

• The muscles work according to laws of mechanical leverage. Thus, we must conform as closely as possible to the Principles of Efficient Muscle Function (see pp. 9 – 11). Contradicting these principles wastes time and effort.

---

Thus, any approach which contradicts how we naturally learn and how we naturally move is not a natural approach.

# The Misuse of "Just Let It Happen"

Teachers sometimes advise students to "let go" and "just let it happen." Correctly used, this advice has merit. Overly cautious students need to be encouraged to discover the limits of their development. Further, advanced students need to learn to push themselves to the edge of their ability during performance — this adds excitement and spontaneity to their playing. Thus, "just let it happen" is useful in the following cases:

**• As a means of testing how much reserve of ability a student has with newly learned music.** This is particularly important in pieces which require a rapid tempo. At rapid tempos, students can no longer consciously control their playing to the extent they did during study and practice. Thus, they must learn to trust the secure habits they've acquired in study and practice. This application of "just let it happen" can be used by students at any level — providing they first develop secure habits through careful aim-directed study and practice.

**• As a way of performing after the student has securely learned the music.** Students who are sufficiently advanced in interpretation and performance development should learn to "just let it happen" in performance. (Musicians sometimes refer to this as "taking chances.") This doesn't imply that advanced students should think of nothing as they perform. Rather, it means that they're free to concentrate mainly on expression — the technical aspects of playing will function mostly by habit.

In a misapplication of the natural approach, however, some teachers have used "just let it happen" as a means for *developing* sustained concentration and technical proficiency. The idea is that, if students just let it happen, the body will take over, allowing students to play in a natural and effortless manner. When misused in this way, "just let it happen" is extremely harmful:

**• It implies that, with the right state of mind, sustained concentration and technical proficiency simply happen.** This, of course, is nonsense. Students will play only as well as the habits they've acquired in practice — if they've acquired habits of insecurity during practice, they'll be equally insecure when they "just let it happen."

**• It's a clear invitation to confusion and error.** Without clear aims, students have no way of knowing what should happen when they "just let it happen."

• **_It's extremely harmful for remedial students._** If remedial students "just let it happen," they'll automatically fall back into their old habits.

∾     ∾     ∾     ∾     ∾     ∾     ∾

Sustained concentration and technical proficiency don't simply happen. Achieving them requires clear aims and well-directed study and practice. Students can "just let it happen" only after they've acquired habits of security and confidence. Thus, the wise teacher will use this advice with discretion.

## Summary

Problems in music pedagogy have arisen not because teachers have sought natural approaches to learning an instrument, but because they haven't correctly defined what "natural" really means. "The natural approach" is frequently misinterpreted to mean learning mainly through imitation and intuition. Some teachers note that we learn our own language this way. Thus, they assert, it's sensible to learn an instrument in the same way.

Those who advocate this interpretation of "natural" overlook two very important facts:

> • **We have no evolutionary background for learning to play a musical instrument — the sustained concentration and physical skill required are entirely beyond our normal experience.**
>
> • **The very fact that we must _study_ to learn an instrument implies that the natural process of imitation and intuition alone isn't enough. Although imitation and intuition have a place in learning an instrument, they must be guided and refined with accurate information.**

If we define "natural" as learning through imitation and intuition alone, then contradictory approaches are inevitable. Thus, defining "natural" in this way ultimately dilutes the word itself — if contradictory approaches are equally natural, then nature is so capricious that "natural" has no meaning.

Nature, however, isn't capricious. Our minds and bodies function according to basic principles, and the definition of "natural" must be based accordingly. Once we recognize these principles, we can accurately determine the most natural approach to learning a musical instrument.

# Economy of Movement

Economy of movement is a concept which receives a great deal of attention in guitar instruction. Simply stated, it holds that guitarists should use the least movement possible when playing. Misinterpretation of this concept has spawned the following harmful technical approaches:

> • *To gain speed and fluency in scales, arpeggios, and the tremolo, the right-hand fingers should be trained to move the shortest distance possible.*

> • *Inactive left-hand fingers should be held as close to the fingerboard as possible.*

Both these approaches directly contradict the Follow-Through Principle. You can prove this for yourself through the following experiment:

❑ **With your right-hand wrist and fingers in their naturally aligned and midrange positions, begin loudly drumming i and m on a tabletop. Move them as rapidly as you can in the most comfortable manner possible.**

❑ **As you continue rapidly drumming, gradually make the movements of i and m smaller. Try to maintain both the same speed and volume as you restrict the motions of i and m.**

❑ **Notice that, as your finger movements become smaller, the tension in your hand increases. As the tension increases, your speed and force of movement will unavoidably decrease.**

*In guitar playing, restricting finger movements yields the same result — the power and speed of the movements will unavoidably decrease.*

Guitarists often misinterpret "economy of movement" in the following ways:

1) Many guitarists assume that the outward appearance of a movement is a reliable measurement of its economy. But this simply is not true. ***Economy of movement can't be measured by the outward appearance of a movement — it can only be measured by the amount of exertion required to execute the movement.***

2) Some guitarists assume that they can consciously influence how muscles coordinate during finger movements. This is also untrue. *We can only control movement — we can't control how muscles coordinate to carry out the movement.* If we direct our fingers to carry out a movement which contradicts any of the Principles of Efficient Muscle Function, no amount of conscious direction will teach the muscles to function more advantageously in that movement.

## Summary

The Follow-Through Principle isn't an opinion — it's a factual statement of how our bodies naturally function. A technical approach which contradicts this principle yields the following drawbacks:

> - **You must work harder to achieve a given level of proficiency.**
>
> - **Your ultimate development is limited.**
>
> - **You may sustain injury.**

***Remember, the only reliable criterion for measuring the economy of a muscular activity is the exertion required to execute the activity.***

# Repetitive Strain Injury (RSI)

Tendonitis, tenosynovitis, and carpal tunnel syndrome all fall under the collective title of "Repetitive Strain Injury" (RSI). Among musicians, RSI occurs most frequently in the hands and arms. It reduces the ability of the afflicted muscles to execute skillful movements. If severe enough, RSI can permanently debilitate the muscles, robbing a musician of the ability to play an instrument.[†]

RSI occurs when muscles are repeatedly operated with a high degree of counter-productive (harmful) tension. Although RSI is commonly attributed to overuse of muscles, this isn't entirely accurate. If your muscles are operating without counterproductive tension, it's unlikely that you'll ever injure them through overuse. The main cause of RSI is the *misuse* of muscles.

RSI is a widespread problem among musicians. One study of 485 orchestral musicians found that 64% reported pain related to their playing.[††] Further, since many afflicted musicians don't recognize the symptoms of RSI, they may never seek treatment. Thus, RSI may be more common than this study suggests.

To better understand RSI, you need to understand the following:

- **What is muscular coordination?**

- **How does counterproductive tension affect muscular coordination?**

- **How does RSI develop?**

---

[†]Although my own experience with RSI occurred 40 years ago, I've never recovered the normal use of my right hand. (A.S.)
[††]H. J. H. Fry, "Incidence of overuse syndrome in the symphony orchestra." *Medical Problems of Performing Artists,* 1: pp. 51-55, 1986.

# *Coordination and Counterproductive Tension*

Muscles can only pull, they can't push. Thus, each joint is controlled by at least two opposing muscles. Simply stated, coordination is the accurate timing and force of pull of opposing muscles. The movements used in playing an instrument require extremely accurate coordination.

But in learning the skillful movements required to play an instrument, musicians don't always develop habits of sufficient coordination. Instead, many musicians acquire habits of thought and movement which cause counterproductive tension. Counterproductive tension is any muscular exertion beyond the minimum amount needed to carry out an activity. It signals that opposing muscles aren't coordinating efficiently. Rather than harmoniously working together, opposing muscles are pulling against each other. Once musicians acquire habits of counterproductive tension, their potential for developing RSI is established.

# *How RSI Develops*

There are three stages in the development of RSI:

> *1) The musician acquires habits of thought and movement which cause counterproductive tension:* Counterproductive tension is caused by technique which forces the muscles into disadvantageous positions and movements, or by emotional stress. Few musicians are taught to recognize counterproductive tension — if they notice it at all, they usually regard it as a normal consequence of playing a musical instrument.
>
> *2) The musician consistently pushes through the symptoms of counterproductive tension:* As time goes by, the musician begins to experience problems. His or her ability to control fine movements begins to deteriorate, and playing becomes less accurate. He or she may notice stiffness and a burning sensation in the involved muscles. If the problem is in the hand, the fingers may quiver slightly after only moderate exertion.

> *These are the warning signs of RSI.* They indicate that the body is struggling to coordinate despite counterproductive tension. But again, since few musicians develop a sensitivity to counterproductive tension, they seldom recognize the real cause of their symptoms. Instead, they assume their technique is "off" and practice harder to correct it.
>
> *3) By trying to forcefully push through the symptoms of counterproductive tension, the musician sustains injury:* The musician is trapped in a vicious circle. The more he or she practices, the worse the symptoms become — the worse the symptoms become, the more he or she practices. Thus, musicians literally practice themselves into RSI.

## Musicians Who Develop RSI

Musicians who develop RSI often share these characteristics:

> • *They compel themselves to practice:* Musicians who develop RSI tend to be highly motivated and hardworking. They set high standards for themselves and practice many hours a day to achieve those standards. Typically, they include students on scholarship[†] and professional musicians who must play to earn a living.
>
> • *They discipline themselves to ignore discomfort as they practice:* Because they're compelled to practice, they learn to push through discomfort and even pain. Thus, they ignore the symptoms of counterproductive tension.

---

[†]Ironically, these students are sometimes accused of malingering. I recall a young student who was experiencing symptoms of RSI. Friends of the student assured me that he had consistently practiced seven or eight hours a day. Yet when I mentioned the student's problem to his teacher, the teacher replied, "Isn't it amazing the excuses some students will make to get out of practicing?"

Unfortunately, this situation is all too common. Musicians tend to deal with technical problems by practicing more. Since they don't recognize when counterproductive tension is causing deterioration of their technique, they continue to repeat the same faulty habits of playing.

Rarely do these musicians realize that they're practicing themselves into serious injury. After years of training, often with a highly respected teacher, they simply don't believe that this type of injury can happen to them. Perhaps a few suspect something is wrong with their playing, and that continuing to play in the same manner may eventually injure them. But they see no better alternative, and to stop playing is unthinkable.

# Questions about RSI

The previous explanation of RSI raises two questions:

*1) If misusing the muscles causes RSI, why do so many musicians contradict the Principles of Efficient Muscle Function, yet never develop RSI?* The answer lies in one or any combination of the following:

- *They don't play very much:* It takes time for counterproductive tension to cause injury. Musicians who play for modest amounts of time simply don't run as high a risk as musicians who consistently play many hours a day.

- *They don't try to push through the symptoms of counterproductive tension:* For whatever reason, when they experience pain, stiffness, or a loss of control, they simply stop playing. Thus, they never drive themselves to the point where injury can occur.

- *They experience relatively little anxiety:* Counterproductive tension caused by anxiety is difficult to measure. Thus, it's theoretically possible for two musicians to have apparently identical technique and practice an equal amount of time, yet for one to develop RSI and not the other. The deciding factor was probably the relative amounts of anxiety experienced by the two musicians.

- *The physical differences between players:* Some people seem to withstand the effects of counterproductive tension better than others. But these physical differences are subtle. Thus, regardless of the ability of their bodies to withstand counterproductive tension, musicians who continually function with such tension may not escape RSI.

**2) Why doesn't fatigue force musicians to stop playing?** For example, athletes who overexert themselves will usually collapse from exhaustion before they sustain RSI. Shouldn't this natural safety device also protect musicians from injury? The answer lies in the following characteristics of muscle activity:

- *The difference between overuse and misuse:* If muscles are operating at or near maximum advantage, the natural safety device works very well — fatigue caused by overuse will force us to stop before we sustain RSI. But if muscles are misused — forced to operate contrary to the Principles of Efficient Muscle Function — this safety device apparently doesn't work well. Although the body does send warnings — fatigue, soreness, cramps, and loss of control — we can push through these warnings and continue to the point where injury occurs.

- *The difference between small-muscle activity and large-muscle activity:* When small muscles become fatigued, the body responds with a natural chain reaction — adjacent larger muscles attempt to compensate for the fatigued small muscles. In large-muscle activities, the muscles simply tire and stop — there are no larger adjacent muscles with which to compensate. Thus, it's easier for the body to continue a small-muscle activity to the point where RSI can occur.

# *Overcoming RSI*

Until now, doctors have been reluctant to question how musicians learn to play. Their reluctance is understandable — musicians themselves often strongly disagree about how technique should be taught. Instead, doctors have attempted to treat RSI by dealing with the condition itself rather than its causes. They've concentrated on trying to cure or at least control RSI through rest, physical therapy, and drugs, even though none of these has proven entirely effective. Thus, neither doctors nor musicians have fully realized that *how* musicians play — both physically and mentally — is directly responsible for RSI.

If you've suffered a severe case of RSI, of course, treatment is necessary. *But diagnosis and treatment by themselves are insufficient: you must also learn to play differently from the technique which caused your disability in the first place.* To avoid further injury, you must do the following:

> • *Develop a sensitivity to counterproductive tension.* The body always gives warnings when it's repeatedly forced to function in disadvantageous positions or movements. Chronic muscular tightness, soreness, cramps, or a loss of control all signal that something's wrong. If any of these symptoms persist, stop playing immediately. Carefully evaluate your technique and approach. Don't wait for severe pain — some victims of RSI lose their ability to play without ever noticing much, if any, pain.
>
> • *Learn new habits of movement which minimize counterproductive tension.* Study the concepts in "The Principles of Efficient Muscle Function," pp. 9–11. Then, after carefully evaluating your technique, begin learning new habits of movement and positioning which enable you to avoid counterproductive tension.
>
> • *Avoid old habits of movement which cause counterproductive tension.* Remember, you're learning new habits of playing. The most efficient way to do this is to consistently emphasize correct habits of movement and positioning. Don't fall back into your old habits of playing.

> • *Eliminate confusion and anxiety.* Confusion and anxiety play a far greater role in RSI than musicians have generally realized. Counterproductive tension caused by confusion and anxiety can be just as harmful as counterproductive tension caused by faulty positioning and movement. Carefully study and apply the concepts in "Approaching Guitar Study," *Part One,* "Memorizing Music," *Part Two,* and "Performance Development," *Part Three.*

## Summary

The best cure for RSI is prevention. By always observing the following as you study and practice, you can virtually eliminate the risk of RSI:

> • Keep your mind and body free from anxiety and illness.
>
> • Have a definite aim of movement.
>
> • Provide maximum advantage for the involved muscles.
>
> • Repeat the movement accurately and without confusion.

*Above all, be sensitive to the signals sent by your body.* If you experience chronic discomfort or a loss of control, it signals that you're misusing your muscles. Stop immediately, then determine and eliminate the cause.

# Avoiding Chronic Shoulder Pain

Precise control of both upper arms is an important part of guitar technique. To carry out accurate movements of the fingers, the upper arm must maintain a position which allows the fingers to function freely. During normal playing, the exertion required to support the upper arm can be accomplished entirely with the muscles controlling the shoulder joint — this is the joint where the upper arm joins the shoulder.

**Chronic shoulder pain occurs when the wrong muscles are brought into play. Most often, it's caused by counterproductive tension in the muscles which lift or lower the entire shoulder area.**

Although pain can occur in either shoulder, right shoulder pain is far more common than left shoulder pain. This is because of the different demands placed on your right and left shoulders during guitar playing. In normal playing, the left shoulder joint remains relatively mobile — the upper arm moves with every left-hand shift. Although it's possible for tension to accumulate in the muscles controlling the entire shoulder, the constant left-hand movement acts as a natural release of this tension. Further, only the left lower arm requires constant support — the upper arm generally assumes a relaxed downward position. Thus, the left shoulder seldom accumulates enough tension to cause pain.

The right shoulder joint position, however, is relatively static — there's not enough movement to cause a natural release of tension. Further, the entire right arm requires constant support. Thus, if the muscles controlling the entire shoulder area become tense, they tend to stay tensed. This tension not only causes pain which can spread to the back, it can also spread down the arms to hinder the free function of the hands.

# *Learning to Recognize Correct Arm Movement*

To avoid chronic shoulder pain, you must acquire the habit of moving your upper arm at the shoulder joint alone — the muscles controlling the shoulder itself should remain relaxed. But these two movements feel so similar that we seldom distinguish between them — indeed, in everyday activities, they often occur simultaneously. Thus, you must first become sensitive to the difference between movement of the entire shoulder and movment at the shoulder joint alone.

The following procedure can be carried out with whichever shoulder has been causing you pain. You'll need a mirror large enough to show your head and torso — you won't need the guitar.

❑ **Face the mirror with your shoulders in a relaxed and naturally rounded position.**

❑ **Lift and drop your shoulder several times — this is movement of the entire shoulder. *The muscles controlling this movement should remain relaxed during normal playing.***

❑ **Allow your shoulder to return to its relaxed position.**

❑ **Now slowly raise and lower your arm to the side several times — this is movement at the shoulder joint. (Watch your shoulder carefully! Don't allow it to rise as you raise your arm.) *The muscles controlling this movement are the ones you'll use to hold your arm in normal playing position.***

Repeat both these movements many times, until you can begin to feel the difference between them.

∞     ∞     ∞     ∞     ∞     ∞     ∞

Left shoulder pain usually begins to disappear once you become aware of the difference between these two movements. For the left shoulder, moving the upper arm from the shoulder joint feels natural enough that you should have little problem acquiring habits of correct movement. Avoiding right-shoulder pain, however, is more challenging. Because you must lift your right upper arm into playing position, lifting the entire shoulder tends to feel very natural. To avoid this harmful movement, you must acquire new habits of playing. The following procedure will help you acquire these new habits.

## Procedure for Training the Right Shoulder

When you've become sensitive to the two different movements with your right arm, you're ready to begin this movement on the guitar. Facing a mirror, sit in normal playing position with the guitar. Before you begin, allow your right arm to hang in a relaxed position at your side. You may wish to shake it loosely — this will help to relax your shoulder muscles. Then carefully place your right arm in playing position. *Don't allow your shoulder to rise!* It should remain in the same relaxed and sloping position as your left shoulder.

Proceed as follows:

❑ **To steady the guitar in playing position during this exercise, grasp the upper bout of the guitar with your left hand.**

❑ **With your fingers curled in a loose fist, lightly place your right hand on the strings. Your hand should rest over the edge of the soundhole nearest the bridge — your wrist should be aligned and arched in its normal playing position.**

❑ ***Moving only from the shoulder joint***, **slide your hand back and forth along the strings. Your wrist should remain normally aligned and arched as you move. Your movements should be large enough for you to clearly feel movement at your shoulder joint — your hand should alternately slide over the fingerboard as far as the 7th fret, and all the way back to the bridge.[†] (Notice that, if your fingers are prepared against the strings, the nails tend to catch on the frets — this is why you should keep your fingers curled in a loose fist.)**

[†]If you're an experienced guitarist, you'll recognize this as the movement used for changing tone color and executing artificial harmonics. Thus, this movement is not only valuable for learning to avoid right shoulder pain — it's also an essential part of guitar technique.

❏ *Watch your right shoulder very carefully!* **If it starts to rise out of its relaxed position, stop immediately. If your shoulder becomes even slightly tense, perform the right-hand position check several times — this helps to relax your shoulder muscles.†**

Perform these steps many times. Concentrate on moving from the shoulder joint alone and keeping the shoulder muscles relaxed. Take frequent breaks to allow your muscles to release. Constantly check your shoulder posture as you execute the right-arm movements — your right shoulder should always remain in the same relaxed and sloping position as your left shoulder.

At first, you may find your forearm pressing against the guitar so hard that it chafes against the rim of the guitar. If so, you're allowing too much of the weight of your arm to press against the guitar. Allow only enough weight to keep the guitar in position — as you move, your forearm should slide comfortably across the area of the soundboard just below the rim of the guitar.

∾     ∾     ∾     ∾     ∾     ∾     ∾

As you become proficient in moving only from the shoulder joint, you'll need to begin incorporating this movement into your playing. The following procedure will help you accomplish this:

❏ **Using the previous procedure, slide your hand back and forth along the strings several times. Then, in a smooth continuation of this movement, carefully slide your hand into normal playing position. NOTE: Sliding your hand into playing position from the fingerboard tends to relax your shoulder — thus it requires little practice. Sliding your hand into playing position from the bridge, however, tends to cause tension in your shoulder — thus, this movement requires far more practice.**

❏ **Using prepared-strokes, sound the strings several times to ensure that your right hand and arm are in a comfortable playing position.**

---

†For a description of the right-hand position check, see p. 14.

❑ **Repeat the previous steps. Aim to slide in and out of normal playing position by moving only from the shoulder joint.**

❑ *Watch your right shoulder!* **As you slide into playing position, you may have a strong tendency to lift your shoulder — don't allow this to happen.**

## *Summary*

Your ability to avoid chronic shoulder pain depends on the following factors:

> • **Your ability to distinguish between movement at the shoulder joint and lifting the entire shoulder.**
>
> • **Your ability to accurately repeat the correct movement — moving from the shoulder joint alone — until it becomes habitual.**
>
> • **Your ability to play — whether practicing or performing — without confusion and error.**

Like all aspects of guitar positioning, eliminating chronic shoulder pain is a gradual and challenging process. You should defer performing during this process — otherwise you'll tend to fall back into the same habits which caused your shoulder pain in the first place. Spend as much time as you need with these procedures. The careful practice you devote to acquiring correct habits of movement will be well rewarded.

*A book combining advanced technique and music reading is currently in preparation. Until it's available, students who've completed both Part One and Part Two of* Learning the Classic Guitar *should continue on to Aaron Shearer's* Classic Guitar Technique, Volume II, *CPP/Belwin, Inc., 15800 N.W. 48th Avenue, Miami, FL 33014.*

# Index